ARKANSAS BUCKET LIST

*Set Off on **120 Epic Adventures** and Discover Incredible Destinations to Live Out Your Dreams While Creating Unforgettable Memories that Will Last a Lifetime.*

(Online Digital MAP included - access it through the link provided in the MAP Chapter of this book)

BeCrePress Travel

table of contents

ARKANSAS BUCKET LIST

TABLE OF CONTENTS

INTRODUCTION 9

ABOUT ARKANSAS 11

    LANDSCAPE OF ARKANSAS.. 11
    FLORA AND FAUNA OF ARKANSAS 12
    CLIMATE OF ARKANSAS.. 13
    HISTORY OF ARKANSAS.. 14

HOW TO USE THIS GUIDE 16

ALTUS 19

    POST WINERY... 19

BELLA VISTA 20

    MILDRED B. COOPER MEMORIAL CHAPEL.................................... 20
    TANYARD CREEK NATURE TRAIL... 20

BENTONVILLE 22

    21C MUSEUM 22
    BENTONVILLE TOWN SQUARE 22
    BUCKYBALL AT CRYSTAL BRIDGES 23
    COMPTON GARDENS AND ARBORETUM 24
    FRANK LLOYD WRIGHT'S BACHMAN-WILSON HOUSE 24
    PEEL MUSEUM & BOTANICAL GARDEN.. 25
    SCOTT FAMILY AMAZEUM 26

BERRYVILLE... 27

    COSMIC CAVERN 27

BISMARCK 28

    DEGRAY LAKE RESORT STATE PARK 28

BULL SHOALS 29

    BULL SHOALS DAM... 29

CLINTON 30

    NATURAL BRIDGE 30

DARDANELLE 31

    MOUNT NEBO STATE PARK 31

ARKANSAS BUCKET LIST

DYESS 32

HISTORIC DYESS COLONY: BOYHOOD HOME OF JOHNNY CASH........................32
JOHNNY CASH HOUSE 32

EUREKA SPRINGS 34

BASIN SPRING PARK 34
BEAVER LAKE 34
BLUE SPRING HERITAGE CENTER 35
EUREKA SPRINGS HISTORICAL DOWNTOWN...36
EUREKA SPRINGS TRANSIT 36
KEELS CREEK WINERY 37
LAKE LEATHERWOOD 37
ONYX CAVE PARK...38
PIVOT ROCK AND NATURAL BRIDGE 39
QUICKSILVER GALLERY...39
QUIGLEY'S CASTLE...40
ST. ELIZABETH'S CATHOLIC CHURCH...40

FAIRFIELD BAY.. 42

FAIRFIELD BAY MARINA..42

FAYETTEVILLE 43

BAUM STADIUM 43
BOTANICAL GARDEN OF THE OZARKS 43
CLINTON HOUSE MUSEUM 44
DONALD W. REYNOLDS RAZORBACK STADIUM 45
LAKE FAYETTEVILLE 45
SQUARE GARDENS 46
THEATRESQUARED 47
WALTON ARTS CENTER 47
WILSON PARK 48

FIFTY SIX 49

BLANCHARD SPRINGS CAVERNS 49

FORT SMITH.. 50

FORT SMITH MUSEUM OF HISTORY 50
FORT SMITH NATIONAL CEMETERY 50
FORT SMITH NATIONAL HISTORIC SITE 51
MISS LAURA'S VISITOR CENTER..52

GARFIELD... 53

ARKANSAS BUCKET LIST

Pea Ridge National Military Park 53

GENTRY **54**

Wild Wilderness Drive-Through Safari 54

GREENBRIER **55**

Woolly Hollow State Park... 55

HARRISON **56**

Triple Falls 56

HEBER SPRINGS **57**

Greers Ferry Lake... 57

HOPE **58**

President William Jefferson Clinton Birthplace Home.. 58

HOT SPRINGS... **59**

Anthony Chapel.. 59
Arkansas Alligator Farm & Petting Zoo.. 59
Buckstaff Bathhouse 60
Funtrackers Family Fun Park 61
Gangster Museum of America 61
Grand Promenade 62
Lake Catherine State Park.. 63
Magic Springs Theme and Water Park 63
Mid-America Science Museum 64
Mountain Valley Spring Water Visitor Center & Museum 65
Pirate's Cove Adventure Golf 65
Superior Bathhouse Brewery and Distillery.. 66
Thai-Me Spa 66
The Galaxy Connection 67
Tiny Town.. 68

JASPER... **69**

Arkansas Grand Canyon 69

JERSEY **70**

Moro Bay State Park.. 70

JONESBORO.. **71**

Craighead Forest Park 71

ARKANSAS BUCKET LIST

Forrest L Wood Crowley's Ridge Nature Center 71

KINGSTON...73

Hawksbill Crag...73
Lost Valley Trail..73

KIRBY 75

Daisy State Park...75

LITTLE ROCK...76

Arkansas Arts Center 76
Arkansas State Capitol..76
Big Dam Bridge..77
Esse Purse Museum & Store...78
H. U. Lee International Gate and Garden...................................78
Historic Arkansas Museum 79
Little Rock Zoo...80
MacArthur Museum of Arkansas Military History 80
Museum Of Discovery..81
Mystery Mansion Escape Room..82
Old State House Museum..82
Pinnacle Mountain State Park 83
River Market District 84
Riverfront Park 84
Rock Town Distillery 85
Simmons Bank Arena 85
The Arkansas River Trail..86
Two Rivers Park 87

MAMMOTH SPRING...88

Mammoth Spring State Park 88

MENA 89

Board Camp Crystal Mine 89
Queen Wilhelmina State Park 89

MORRILTON...91

Cedar Falls Trail 91
Petit Jean State Park..91

MOUNT IDA 93

Twin Creek Crystal Mine 93

WEGNER QUARTZ CRYSTAL MINES 93

MOUNT IDA 95

LAKE OUACHITA 95

MOUNTAIN VIEW 96

BLANCHARD SPRINGS RECREATION AREA 96
OZARK FOLK CENTER STATE PARK 96

MOUNTAINBURG 98

LAKE FORT SMITH STATE PARK 98

MURFREESBORO 99

KA DO HA INDIAN VILLAGE 99

NORTH LITTLE ROCK 100

ARKANSAS INLAND MARITIME MUSEUM 100
BURNS PARK 100
DICKEY-STEPHENS PARK 101
JUNCTION BRIDGE 101
THE OLD MILL 102

ODEN 104

OUACHITA NATIONAL FOREST 104

PARIS 105

MOUNT MAGAZINE STATE PARK 105

PRAIRIE GROVE 106

PRAIRIE GROVE BATTLEFIELD STATE PARK 106

ROGERS 107

DAISY AIRGUN MUSEUM 107
HOBBS STATE PARK CONSERVATION AREA 107
WAR EAGLE CAVERN ON BEAVER LAKE 108
WAR EAGLE MILL GENERAL STORE 109
P. ALLEN SMITH'S GARDEN HOME 109

RUSSELLVILLE 111

LAKE DARDENELLE STATE PARK 111

SPRINGDALE 112

ARKANSAS BUCKET LIST

Arvest Ballpark 112

Sassafras Springs Vineyard 112

Tontitown Winery...113

ST JOE.. **114**

Buffalo National River Park 114

MAP **115**

INTRODUCTION

Welcome to "Arkansas Bucket List: Set Off on 120 Epic Adventures and Discover Incredible Destinations to Live Out Your Dreams." This guide is your passport to the most enchanting and thrilling destinations across the Natural State, curated to ignite your sense of adventure and curiosity.

Arkansas, with its rich tapestry of landscapes, flora and fauna, diverse climate, and fascinating history, promises a journey filled with unforgettable memories and experiences.

Each destination within this guide is meticulously detailed to ensure you have all the information you need for a seamless and enriching visit. You will find:

- A vivid description: Immerse yourself in the essence of each location, painted with words to spark your imagination and excitement.

- The address: To ensure you arrive at the right place without any confusion.

- The nearest city: Helping you to orient yourself and understand the broader geographical context.

- GPS coordinates: Precise coordinates ready to be entered into your device for easy navigation.

- The best time to visit: Maximize your experience by knowing when each destination is at its peak.

- Tolls and access fees: Clear information on any costs associated with your visit, so there are no surprises.

- Did you know?: Fascinating trivia to enrich your knowledge and appreciation of each site.

- Website: Stay updated with the latest information directly from each destination's official site.

As an added bonus, we've included an interactive State Map with all the destinations pre-loaded. This digital compass will guide you effortlessly from one adventure to the next, making your exploration of Arkansas smooth and stress-free.

Imagine wandering through the picturesque vineyards of Post Winery, marveling at the scenic beauty of Greers Ferry Lake, or standing in awe beneath the towering bluffs of Hawksbill Crag. Picture yourself discovering the serene trails of Lost Valley, the cascading beauty of Triple Falls, and the architectural wonder of Mildred B. Cooper Memorial Chapel. From the vibrant Bentonville Town Square to the historical richness of the Johnny Cash House, each destination invites you to dive deep into the heart of Arkansas.

Get ready to embrace the natural splendor, cultural richness, and historical depth of Arkansas. This guide is not just about visiting places; it's about living out dreams, creating lasting memories, and writing your own epic tale in the enchanting landscape of Arkansas. So, polish your hiking boots, charge your camera, and let the adventures begin. Your unforgettable journey through the Natural State awaits.

ABOUT ARKANSAS

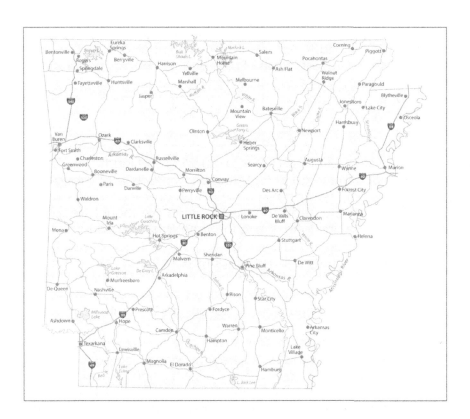

Landscape of Arkansas

Nestled in the heart of the American South, Arkansas boasts a landscape that is as diverse as it is enchanting, painting a vivid picture of natural splendor. From the rolling hills of the Ozarks to the flat plains of the Mississippi Delta, the state's topography is a mesmerizing blend of mountains, forests, rivers, and lakes that beckon adventurers and nature lovers alike.

The Ozark Mountains in the northwest present a rugged beauty, with limestone bluffs, deep valleys, and swift rivers carving their way through the land. This region is a haven for outdoor enthusiasts, offering opportunities for hiking, rock climbing, and exploring hidden caverns. The lush, dense forests that cloak these mountains create a verdant canopy, teeming with wildlife and a rich array of flora.

Central Arkansas introduces the Ouachita Mountains, where the terrain shifts to rolling ridges and clear, flowing streams. The Ouachitas are unique in their east-west orientation, a geological rarity that adds to their allure. Here, vast forests of pine and hardwoods stretch out as far as the eye can see, offering a serene retreat into nature. This area is also home to thermal springs, adding a touch of mystical charm to the landscape.

The Arkansas River Valley bisects the state, its wide, fertile plains providing a stark contrast to the surrounding highlands. This river, a vital artery of commerce and recreation, winds its way through the heart of Arkansas, flanked by lush wetlands and verdant farmlands. The valley is punctuated by majestic peaks like Mount Nebo and Mount Magazine, the latter being the state's highest point.

To the east, the Mississippi Delta's expansive flatlands stretch towards the horizon, rich with agricultural bounty and steeped in cultural history. This region's landscape is defined by its wide, slow-moving rivers and an intricate network of bayous and swamps, home to a diverse ecosystem.

In the southern part of the state, the Timberlands' dense forests and numerous lakes and streams offer a pristine wilderness experience. Here, the landscape is dotted with sparkling bodies of water such as Lake Ouachita, one of the cleanest lakes in the country, providing idyllic settings for boating, fishing, and swimming.

Arkansas' landscape is a dynamic tapestry of natural wonders, each region offering its own unique charm and adventure. Whether you're drawn to the rugged peaks of the Ozarks, the tranquil forests of the Ouachitas, the fertile valleys along the Arkansas River, or the rich, flat deltas of the east, Arkansas promises a captivating journey through some of the most beautiful and diverse scenery in the United States.

Flora and Fauna of Arkansas

Arkansas is a state of lush forests, vibrant flora, and diverse fauna, painting a picture of natural splendor. The state is divided into three broad ecoregions: the Ozark, Ouachita-Appalachian Forests, the Mississippi Alluvial and Southeast USA Coastal Plains, and the Southeastern USA Plains. Dominant tree species include oak, hickory, shortleaf pine, and loblolly pine. In the eastern bayous, cypress and water oaks thrive, while the northwestern highlands are home to Ozark white cedars, dogwoods, and redbuds.

The wildlife in Arkansas is equally captivating, featuring white-tailed deer, elk, and the iconic bald eagle. The state's waterways and wetlands support a rich array of bird species, making it a haven for bird watchers. The varied landscapes, from the dense pine forests of the south to the hardwood forests of the highlands, offer habitats for numerous species, creating a biodiversity hotspot.

The Arkansas River Valley and the Mississippi Delta provide a mosaic of habitats supporting diverse plant and animal life. From the vibrant spring blooms of dogwoods and redbuds to the autumn hues of oak and hickory, Arkansas's flora paints a dynamic and colorful landscape throughout the year. The state's natural beauty is a testament to its rich ecological heritage, inviting nature enthusiasts to explore its forests, mountains, and wetlands, each teeming with life and beauty.

Climate of Arkansas

Arkansas boasts a humid subtropical climate, characterized by hot, humid summers and mild to cool winters. Summers in Arkansas are typically long and hot, with July temperatures averaging around 93°F (34°C) in Little Rock, while the northwest regions like Siloam Springs enjoy slightly cooler temperatures. Winters are generally mild, with January highs around 51°F (11°C) in Little Rock and colder temperatures in the northwest.

The state receives ample rainfall, averaging between 40 to 60 inches annually, contributing to its lush landscapes. Arkansas also experiences a variety of extreme weather, including thunderstorms, tornadoes, and occasional ice storms, adding a dynamic element to its climate.

This blend of weather conditions ensures that Arkansas remains vibrant and green throughout the year, supporting a rich diversity of plant and animal life. The state's climate, with its warm and inviting summers and gentle, crisp winters, provides the perfect backdrop for exploring its natural beauty, from the rolling hills of the Ozarks to the fertile plains of the Mississippi Delta. The ever-changing weather patterns and the state's readiness for occasional extremes add a touch of adventure and excitement, making Arkansas a compelling destination for nature enthusiasts and adventure seekers alike.

Whether basking in the summer sun by Greers Ferry Lake or witnessing the serene winter landscapes, the climate of Arkansas enhances the allure of its beautiful destinations.

History of Arkansas

Arkansas' history is a captivating tale of resilience, exploration, and cultural transformation. Long before European explorers arrived, indigenous tribes like the Quapaw, Osage, and Caddo thrived in the region, their legacies woven into the state's cultural fabric.

The first European to set foot in Arkansas was Spanish explorer Hernando de Soto in 1541, followed by French explorers Jacques Marquette and Louis Jolliet in 1673. Robert La Salle's expedition in 1681 led to the establishment of Arkansas Post, the first European settlement in the territory.

The Louisiana Purchase of 1803 integrated Arkansas into the United States, and it became the Territory of Arkansaw in 1819. Statehood followed in 1836, marking the beginning of a new era. The 19th century saw Arkansas's economy heavily reliant on cotton and enslaved labor, setting the stage for its significant role in the Civil War. Arkansas seceded from the Union in 1861, joining the Confederacy, but was readmitted to the Union in 1868 during Reconstruction.

The late 19th and early 20th centuries brought rapid change, with railroads expanding trade and the growth of towns. Arkansas became a pivotal site during the Civil Rights Movement, notably during the 1957 integration of Little Rock Central High School. The bravery of the Little Rock Nine, who faced violent resistance as they sought to attend the previously all-white school, marked a significant chapter in the fight for civil rights.

Throughout its history, Arkansas has been shaped by its diverse cultures and resilient spirit.

From its indigenous roots and colonial past to its role in the Civil War and the Civil Rights Movement, the state's rich historical tapestry is a testament to its enduring significance. This vibrant past continues to influence its present, making Arkansas a place of profound historical depth and cultural richness, inviting visitors to explore its storied landscapes and the narratives they hold.

How to Use this Guide

Welcome to your comprehensive guide to exploring Arkansas! This chapter is dedicated to helping you understand how to effectively use this guide and the interactive map to enhance your travel experience. Let's dive into the simple steps to navigate the book and utilize the digital tools provided, ensuring you have the best adventure possible.

Understanding the Guide's Structure

The guide features 120 of the best destinations across the beautiful state of Arkansas, thoughtfully compiled to inspire and facilitate your explorations. These destinations are divided into areas and listed alphabetically. This organization aims to simplify your search process, making it quick and intuitive to locate each destination in the book.

Using the Alphabetical Listings

Since the destination areas are arranged alphabetically, you can easily flip through the guide to find a specific place or browse areas that catch your interest. Each destination entry in the book includes essential information such as:

- A vivid description of the destination.

- The complete address and the nearest major city, giving you a quick geographical context.

- GPS coordinates for precise navigation.

- The best times to visit, helping you plan your trip according to seasonal attractions and weather.

- Details on tolls or access fees, preparing you for any costs associated with your visit.

- Fun trivia to enhance your knowledge and appreciation of each location.

- A link to the official website for up-to-date information.

To further enhance your experience and save time, you can scan these website links using apps like Google Lens to open them directly without the need to type them into a browser. This seamless integration allows for quicker access to the latest information and resources about each destination.

Navigating with the Interactive State Map

Your guide comes equipped with an innovative tool—an interactive map of Arkansas that integrates seamlessly with Google Maps. This digital map is pre-loaded with all 120 destinations, offering an effortless way to visualize and plan your journey across the state.

How to Use the Map:

- **Open the Interactive Map**: Start by accessing the digital map through the link provided in your guide. You can open it on any device that supports Google Maps, such as a smartphone, tablet, or computer.

- **Choose Your Starting Point:** Decide where you will begin your adventure. You might start from your current location or another specific point in Arkansas.

- **Explore Nearby Destinations:** With the map open, zoom in and out to view the destinations near your starting point. Click on any marker to see a brief description and access quick links for navigation and more details.

- **Plan Your Itinerary:** Based on the destinations close to your chosen start, you can create a personalized itinerary. You can select multiple locations to visit in a day or plan a more extended road trip through various regions.

Combining the Book and Map for Best Results

To get the most out of your adventures:

- Cross-Reference: Use the interactive map to spot destinations you are interested in and then refer back to the guidebook for detailed information and insights.

- Plan Sequentially: As you plan your route on the map, use the alphabetical listing in the book to easily gather information on each destination and organize your visits efficiently.

- Stay Updated: Regularly check the provided website links for any changes in operation hours, fees, or special events at the destinations.

By following these guidelines and utilizing both the guidebook and the interactive map, you will be well-equipped to explore Arkansas's diverse landscapes and attractions. Whether you are seeking solitude in nature, adventure in the outdoors, or cultural experiences in urban settings, this guide will serve as your reliable companion, ensuring every adventure is memorable and every discovery is enriching. Happy travels!

ALTUS

Post Winery

Find your sense of adventure and flavor at Post Winery, the oldest vineyard in Arkansas nestled in the charming town of Altus. This family-owned establishment has been producing award-winning wines since 1872, offering visitors a taste of tradition and innovation.

Located on Saint Marys Mountain, this vineyard provides a picturesque backdrop for wine enthusiasts. As you explore the estate, you can indulge in wine tastings, tour the winery, and learn about the winemaking process.

The unique feature here is the opportunity to savor locally crafted wines while enjoying stunning views of the Arkansas River Valley.

Location: 1700 Saint Marys Mountain Rd, Altus, AR 72821-9001

Closest City or Town: Altus, Arkansas

How to Get There: Accessible via US-64 W; take the exit towards Altus from I-40, then follow the signs to Saint Marys Mountain Road.

GPS Coordinates: 35.4482839° N, 93.7602934° W

Best Time to Visit: Year-round, but fall offers the best vineyard views

Pass/Permit/Fees: Free to enter; wine tasting and tours have fees

Did You Know? Post Winery is famed for its muscadine wine, a true Southern classic.

Website: http://www.postwinery.com/

BELLA VISTA

Mildred B. Cooper Memorial Chapel

Find your sense of wonder at the Mildred B. Cooper Memorial Chapel, a breathtaking architectural gem in Bella Vista, Arkansas. This enchanting chapel, designed by renowned architect E. Fay Jones, offers an immersive experience set amidst the serene beauty of the Ozark woods. With its soaring steel and glass construction, the chapel invites visitors to relax and reflect in harmony with nature. Located within Blowing Springs Park, it serves as a peaceful sanctuary, perfect for moments of introspection or even intimate ceremonies.

Location: 504 Memorial Dr, Bella Vista, AR 72714-1842

Closest City or Town: Bella Vista, Arkansas

How to Get There: From I-49 N, take exit 93 and merge onto US-71 N. Continue on US-71 N until you reach Bella Vista, then follow signs for Blowing Springs Park.

GPS Coordinates: 36.4770521° N, 94.2444731° W

Best Time to Visit: Spring and fall offer vibrant foliage and comfortable weather.

Pass/Permit/Fees: Free to enter.

Did You Know? The chapel is designed to blend seamlessly with its natural surroundings, creating a spiritual experience in the heart of nature.

Website: https://www.cooperchapel.com/

Tanyard Creek Nature Trail

Reconnect with nature on the picturesque Tanyard Creek Nature Trail, a hidden gem in Bella Vista, Arkansas. This mile-long loop trail offers a serene setting for hiking, birdwatching, and fishing, making it a delightful escape for outdoor enthusiasts. Nestled in the rolling hills, the trail features a charming waterfall, wooden bridges, and scenic views that invite visitors to embrace the tranquility of the outdoors.

Location: 34 Cannock Ln, Bella Vista, AR 72715

Closest City or Town: Bella Vista, Arkansas

How to Get There: From I-49 N, take exit 93 and merge onto US-71 N. Turn left onto Oldham Dr, then follow signs to Tanyard Creek.

GPS Coordinates: 36.4718824° N, 94.2609679° W

Best Time to Visit: Spring and early summer for the lush greenery and waterfall views.

Pass/Permit/Fees: Free to access.

Did You know? The trail was developed and maintained by local volunteers, making it a true community treasure.

Website: https://en.wikipedia.org/wiki/Tanyard_Creek_(Arkansas)

BENTONVILLE

21c Museum

Immerse yourself in contemporary art at the 21c Museum in Bentonville, Arkansas, where innovative exhibits blend seamlessly with boutique luxury. This unique destination offers an eclectic collection of art installations, interactive displays, and thought-provoking pieces that captivate the imagination. Located in the heart of Bentonville's historic district, the 21c Museum Hotel combines art, culture, and hospitality, offering an unparalleled experience.

Location: 200 NE a St, Bentonville, AR 72712-5360

Closest City or Town: Bentonville, Arkansas

How to Get There: Easily accessible from I-49 N. Take exit 93 for US-71 N, continuing onto Bentonville. Follow signs to the 21c Museum.

GPS Coordinates: 36.3749519° N, 94.2073192° W

Best Time to Visit: Year-round, offering new exhibits throughout the year.

Pass/Permit/Fees: Free to view exhibits.

Did You Know? The 21c Museum was named one of the best new hotels in the world by Condé Nast Traveler.

Website: http://www.21cmuseumhotels.com/bentonville/museum/

Bentonville Town Square

Experience the charm of Bentonville Town Square, a quaint and vibrant hub that captures the essence of small-town America. Surrounded by boutique shops, cozy cafes, and historic buildings, the square is a perfect spot to explore local culture. Don't miss the bustling farmers' market, seasonal events, and public art installations that make every visit unique.

Location: 103 S Main St, Bentonville, AR 72712

Closest City or Town: Bentonville, Arkansas

How to Get There: From I-49 N, take exit 93 towards Bentonville. Follow Central Ave to S Main St to reach the square.

GPS Coordinates: 36.3721261° N, 94.2087103° W

Best Time to Visit: Spring through fall for outdoor events and markets.

Pass/Permit/Fees: Free to explore.

Did You Know? Bentonville Town Square is the birthplace of Walmart, where Sam Walton opened his original Five and Dime store.

Website: https://www.downtownbentonville.org/explore/the-square

Buckyball at Crystal Bridges

Marvel at the mesmerizing Buckyball at Crystal Bridges Museum of American Art in Bentonville, Arkansas. This stunning geometric sculpture, designed by artist Leo Villareal, comes to life at dusk with an LED light display that mesmerizes visitors. Nestled within the museum's picturesque grounds, the Buckyball offers a captivating blend of art and technology, providing an unforgettable evening experience.

Location: 600 Museum Way, Crystal Bridges Museum of American Art, Bentonville, AR 72712-4947

Closest City or Town: Bentonville, Arkansas

How to Get There: Accessible via I-49 N. Take exit 93 for Bentonville and follow signs to Crystal Bridges Museum.

GPS Coordinates: 36.3782210° N, 94.1986276° W

Best Time to Visit: Evening to witness the full effect of the LED light display.

Pass/Permit/Fees: Free to view.

Did You Know? The Buckyball was inspired by the geodesic spheres of architect Buckminster Fuller and features over 180 LED lights.

Website: http://crystalbridges.org/trails-and-grounds/buckyball/

Compton Gardens and Arboretum

Find your serenity amidst nature at Compton Gardens and Arboretum, a lush retreat located in Bentonville, Arkansas. This beautiful garden and arboretum serve as a living tribute to Dr. Neil Compton, a devoted environmentalist and champion of the Buffalo River. Wander through the winding trails and discover more than six acres of native flora and lush green spaces that provide a peaceful sanctuary for visitors. Located just a stone's throw from the vibrant downtown area, Compton Gardens is Bentonville's hidden gem for nature lovers and plant enthusiasts.

Location: 312 N Main St, Bentonville, AR 72712-5337

Closest City or Town: Bentonville, Arkansas

How to Get There: From US-71, take the exit toward Bentonville. Follow Main Street downtown, and you'll find the gardens on the north end of Main Street.

GPS Coordinates: 36.3766381° N, 94.2081830° W

Best Time to Visit: Spring and summer, when the flowers are in full bloom.

Pass/Permit/Fees: Free to visit.

Did You Know? The garden is home to several Champion Trees, which are the largest of their species in the state of Arkansas.

Website: http://www.peelcompton.org/spaces/visit-compton-gardens/

Frank Lloyd Wright's Bachman-Wilson House

Step into an architectural marvel at Frank Lloyd Wright's Bachman-Wilson House, perfectly nestled at Crystal Bridges Museum of American Art in Bentonville, Arkansas. This exquisite house, originally built in New Jersey in 1954, was meticulously relocated to Arkansas in 2015, preserving Wright's vision and design philosophy. Appreciate the intricate details of this Usonian home, characterized by open floor plans and seamless integration with the surrounding landscape. Located in the heart of the museum's 120-acre grounds, this masterpiece is a must-see for architecture and art lovers alike.

Location: 600 Museum Way at Crystal Bridges Museum of American Art, Bentonville, AR 72712-4947

Closest City or Town: Bentonville, Arkansas

How to Get There: From I-49, take exit 88 for AR-72 toward Bentonville/Rogers. Follow Museum Way to Crystal Bridges.

GPS Coordinates: 36.3804339° N, 94.2040347° W

Best Time to Visit: Year-round, but spring and fall offer the most pleasant weather.

Pass/Permit/Fees: Included with museum admission or free with museum membership.

Did You Know? The house's relocation project spanned over 1,200 miles and took nearly two years to complete.

Website: http://crystalbridges.org/

Peel Museum & Botanical Garden

Immerse yourself in history and horticulture at the Peel Museum & Botanical Garden, a captivating destination in Bentonville, Arkansas. This beautifully restored 1875 mansion serves as a museum showcasing the Victorian-era lifestyle of Colonel Samuel West Peel's family. Tour the elegant rooms filled with period furnishings, then step outside to explore the meticulously maintained botanical gardens that span over two acres. Located just off Walton Boulevard, this destination provides a perfect blend of history and nature, making it a captivating stop for visitors of all ages.

Location: 400 S Walton Blvd, Bentonville, AR 72712-5705

Closest City or Town: Bentonville, Arkansas

How to Get There: From I-49, take exit 85 toward AR-12/AR-102/Bentonville. Follow S Walton Boulevard to the museum.

GPS Coordinates: 36.3691415° N, 94.2222744° W

Best Time to Visit: Spring and fall for garden tours, year-round for museum access.

Pass/Permit/Fees: Admission fees apply; discounts available for children and seniors.

Did You Know? The gardens feature a diverse collection of plants, including several heirloom roses.

Website: http://www.peelcompton.org/spaces/visit-peel/

Scott Family Amazeum

Unleash your inner child at the Scott Family Amazeum, an interactive museum teeming with hands-on exhibits and activities in Bentonville, Arkansas. Designed to spark curiosity and creativity, this innovative space caters to children and adults alike with its science, technology, engineering, arts, and math (STEAM) exhibits. Discover the Tinkering Studio, climb the indoor tree canopy, or splash around in the Water Amazements exhibit. Conveniently located near Crystal Bridges Museum of American Art, the Amazeum offers an ideal adventure for families.

Location: 1009 Museum Way, Bentonville, AR 72712-5176

Closest City or Town: Bentonville, Arkansas

How to Get There: From I-49, take exit 88 for AR-72 toward Bentonville/Rogers. Follow directions to Museum Way.

GPS Coordinates: 36.3792651° N, 94.1972716° W

Best Time to Visit: Year-round, with special events held throughout the year.

Pass/Permit/Fees: Admission fees apply; memberships available for unlimited access.

Did You Know? The museum's interactive exhibits are designed to reflect the region's unique culture and environment.

Website: http://www.amazeum.org/

BERRYVILLE

Cosmic Cavern

Venture below the surface and explore the wonders of Cosmic Cavern, one of the largest privately owned show caves in Arkansas located in Berryville. With two splendid underground lakes, and formations that have been growing for over a million years, this cave promises an awe-inspiring adventure. Take the guided tours that delve deep into this natural marvel, revealing the spectacular beauty and history hidden beneath the earth's surface. Nestled in the Ozarks, Cosmic Cavern offers a mesmerizing journey into the enigmatic underground world.

Location: 6386 AR-21, Berryville, AR 72616

Closest City or Town: Berryville, Arkansas

How to Get There: From US-62, head south on AR-21 for about 7 miles until you reach the cave entrance.

GPS Coordinates: 36.4358276° N, 93.4972525° W

Best Time to Visit: Year-round, with a constant cave temperature making it a great escape in any season.

Pass/Permit/Fees: Guided tour fees apply; visit the website for details.

Did You Know? The cavern's unique Silent Splendor formation is one of the largest soda straws in the Ozarks.

Website: http://www.cosmiccavern.com/

BISMARCK

DeGray Lake Resort State Park

Discover the perfect blend of relaxation and adventure at DeGray Lake Resort State Park, a stunning destination offering endless outdoor activities. Nestled in the foothills of the Ouachita Mountains, this park surrounds the pristine DeGray Lake, providing visitors with a scenic backdrop for their adventures. Enjoy boating, fishing, and swimming in the crystal-clear waters, or explore the numerous hiking and biking trails that wind through the lush forest.

Located in Bismarck, this park is a paradise for nature lovers and thrill-seekers alike. Take advantage of the 18-hole championship golf course, or embark on a wildlife-watching excursion. The park's unique feature is the opportunity to stay at Arkansas's only resort state park lodge, offering comfortable accommodations with stunning lake views.

Location: 2027 State Park Maintenance Rd, Bismarck, AR 71929-7308

Closest City or Town: Bismarck, Arkansas

How to Get There: From I-30, take Exit 78 for AR-84 W toward Bismarck. Continue on AR-84 W and follow signs to DeGray Lake Resort State Park.

GPS Coordinates: 34.2511202° N, 93.1538630° W

Best Time to Visit: Spring and summer for outdoor activities

Pass/Permit/Fees: Varies by activity; some amenities may have fees

Did You Know? DeGray Lake Resort State Park is home to Arkansas's only resort state park lodge with conference center facilities.

Website: http://www.degray.com/

BULL SHOALS

Bull Shoals Dam

Experience the awe-inspiring engineering marvel of Bull Shoals Dam, a must-visit destination for history buffs and nature enthusiasts. Spanning the White River, this massive structure creates Bull Shoals Lake, one of the largest lakes in Arkansas. Enjoy panoramic views from the dam overlook and explore the surrounding park areas.

Located in Bull Shoals, this dam offers a variety of activities such as boating, fishing, and hiking. The visitor center provides educational exhibits about the dam's construction and its impact on the region. The unique feature here is the chance to take guided tours inside the dam, revealing its intricate inner workings.

Location: 153 Dam Overlook Ln, Bull Shoals, AR 72619-2845

Closest City or Town: Bull Shoals, Arkansas

How to Get There: From US-412, take AR-178 W toward Bull Shoals. Follow AR-178 W to Dam Overlook Ln.

GPS Coordinates: 36.3679736° N, 92.5766380° W

Best Time to Visit: Spring through fall for water activities

Pass/Permit/Fees: Free to visit; some activities may have fees

Did You Know? Bull Shoals Dam was once the fifth-largest concrete dam in the world.

Website: http://www.arkansasstateparks.com/bullshoalswhiteriver

CLINTON

Natural Bridge

Step back in time and marvel at the Natural Bridge, a geological wonder that captivates visitors with its stunning beauty. Formed over millions of years, this natural rock arch stands as a testament to the power of erosion. Located near Clinton, the Natural Bridge offers a serene escape into nature, surrounded by picturesque forests and trails.

This unique destination invites you to explore its ancient formation and enjoy the peaceful surroundings. Walk across the bridge, take in the panoramic views, and immerse yourself in the tranquil atmosphere. The highlight of this site is the sheer size and majesty of the rock formation, making it a perfect spot for photography and contemplation.

Location: 1120 Natural Bridge Road, Clinton, AR 72031

Closest City or Town: Clinton, Arkansas

How to Get There: From US-65, take AR-16 W towards Clinton. Follow signs for Natural Bridge Road.

GPS Coordinates: 35.6564150° N, 92.4488051° W

Best Time to Visit: Spring and fall for comfortable weather

Pass/Permit/Fees: Fee for entrance

Did You Know? Natural Bridge has been a tourist attraction since the early 1900s.

Website: https://www.nps.gov/places/natural-bridge-lost-valley-trail.htm

DARDANELLE

Mount Nebo State Park

Embark on an unforgettable adventure at Mount Nebo State Park, where breathtaking vistas and exhilarating trails await. Perched atop Mount Nebo, this park offers panoramic views of the Arkansas River Valley and the surrounding mountains. Located near Dardanelle, it's an ideal destination for outdoor enthusiasts and nature lovers.

Hike or bike the numerous trails, ranging from easy walks to challenging climbs, and experience the park's diverse flora and fauna. The unique feature of Mount Nebo is its 1,350-foot elevation, providing spectacular sunrises and sunsets. Don't miss the chance to explore the historic sites within the park, including old homesteads and remnants of the past.

Location: 16728 W State Highway 155, Dardanelle, AR 72834-8709

Closest City or Town: Dardanelle, Arkansas

How to Get There: From I-40, take Exit 81 for AR-7 S toward Russellville/Dardanelle. Continue on AR-7 S, then follow AR-155 up the mountain.

GPS Coordinates: 35.2185729° N, 93.2527448° W

Best Time to Visit: Spring and fall for mild weather and vibrant foliage

Pass/Permit/Fees: Free to enter; cabin rentals and some activities may have fees

Did You Know? Mount Nebo's name is thought to be inspired by the biblical Mount Nebo where Moses viewed the Promised Land.

Website: http://www.arkansasstateparks.com/mountnebo

DYESS

Historic Dyess Colony: Boyhood Home of Johnny Cash

Journey into the past and explore the Historic Dyess Colony, where the legendary Johnny Cash spent his formative years. This fascinating destination offers a glimpse into the early life of the iconic musician. Located in Dyess, the colony features the restored boyhood home of Johnny Cash, along with a museum and exhibits detailing the history of the New Deal agricultural resettlement community.

Visitors can tour the Cash family home, see personal artifacts, and learn about the challenges and triumphs of the families who lived there. The unique feature of this site is the authentic recreation of Johnny Cash's early environment, providing a deep connection to his music and legacy.

Location: 108 Center Dr, Dyess, AR 72330-8004

Closest City or Town: Dyess, Arkansas

How to Get There: From I-55, take Exit 41 for AR-77 N toward Luxora. Follow AR-77 N and signs for Dyess.

GPS Coordinates: 35.5974351° N, 90.2449764° W

Best Time to Visit: Spring and fall for mild weather

Pass/Permit/Fees: Entrance fees apply

Did You Know? Dyess Colony was established in 1934 as part of President Franklin D. Roosevelt's New Deal program to help poor farmers.

Website: http://dyesscash.astate.edu/

Johnny Cash House

Step into the humble beginnings of a music legend at the Johnny Cash House in Dyess, Arkansas. Explore the boyhood home of the Man in Black, where Johnny Cash's story began. Located in the Arkansas Delta, this historical site offers a detailed glimpse into his early life and the influence of his upbringing. Wander through the restored house, envision the young Cash's daily life, and learn about his rise to fame through various exhibits.

Location: 4791 W County Road 924, Dyess, AR 72330-9671

Closest City or Town: Dyess, Arkansas

How to Get There: Accessible via I-55, take exit 41 to join AR-14 E towards Dyess. Follow local signs to reach County Road 924.

GPS Coordinates: 35.5973924° N, 90.2449937° W

Best Time to Visit: Spring and fall for the most pleasant weather.

Pass/Permit/Fees: Admission fees apply; check the website for details.

Did You Know? Johnny Cash's childhood home was part of a New Deal agricultural colony established during the Great Depression.

Website: http://dyesscash.astate.edu/

EUREKA SPRINGS

Basin Spring Park

Discover a lush, serene escape in the heart of Eureka Springs at Basin Spring Park. Located next to the historic Basin Park Hotel, this green oasis offers visitors a spot to relax and enjoy live music, seasonal festivals, and vibrant gardens. Tucked away in the Arkansas Ozarks, the park is a central hub for community events and a perfect place to appreciate the town's charm.

Location: 3 Spring St Next to Basin Park Hotel, Eureka Springs, AR 72632-3104

Closest City or Town: Eureka Springs, Arkansas

How to Get There: From US-62, head towards the historic downtown area and follow signs to Spring Street.

GPS Coordinates: 36.4019754° N, 93.7373893° W

Best Time to Visit: Spring through fall for the best outdoor events.

Pass/Permit/Fees: Free to enter.

Did You Know? Basin Spring Park was historically known for its healing spring waters, attracting visitors seeking natural remedies.

Website:
http://www.lakeleatherwoodcitypark.com/basinspringpark.htm

Beaver Lake

Enjoy endless outdoor adventures at Beaver Lake, a stunning reservoir near Eureka Springs. Encompassing over 28,000 acres of clear, blue waters, this lake is a paradise for boating, fishing, swimming, and camping. Surrounded by the scenic Ozarks, Beaver Lake offers opportunities for hiking, birdwatching, and simply relaxing by the water.

Location: 4022 Mundell Rd, Eureka Springs, AR 72631-8911

Closest City or Town: Eureka Springs, Arkansas

How to Get There: From US-62, take Mundell Road to reach the lake.

GPS Coordinates: 36.3898295° N, 93.8768171° W

Best Time to Visit: Summer for water activities; fall for picturesque foliage.

Pass/Permit/Fees: Access to the lake is free; fees apply for specific amenities.

Did You Know? Beaver Lake is home to some of the best striped bass fishing in the region.

Website: https://www.recreation.gov/camping/gateways/530

Blue Spring Heritage Center

Step into a world of natural beauty and rich history at Blue Spring Heritage Center in Eureka Springs. This unique destination offers stunning landscapes, historic structures, and the beautiful Blue Spring, which gushes 38 million gallons of water daily. Walk the lush gardens, explore the heritage site, and take in the serenity of this ancient spring.

Location: 1537 Co Rd 210, Eureka Springs, AR 72632-9418

Closest City or Town: Eureka Springs, Arkansas

How to Get There: From US-62, follow local signs to County Road 210 to reach the heritage center.

GPS Coordinates: 36.4657135° N, 93.8130188° W

Best Time to Visit: Spring and summer for the fullest blooms and lush scenery.

Pass/Permit/Fees: Admission fees apply; visit the website for more information.

Did You Know? The site was a significant Native American settlement for thousands of years due to the area's abundant natural resources.

Website: http://www.bluespringheritage.com/

Eureka Springs Historical Downtown

Travel back in time as you stroll through Eureka Springs Historical Downtown. Known for its Victorian architecture, eclectic shops, and vibrant art scene, this charming district offers a delightful mix of history and modern attractions. Don't miss the unique boutiques, art galleries, and delicious eateries that line the narrow, winding streets.

Location: 3 Spring Street, Eureka Springs, AR 72632

Closest City or Town: Eureka Springs, Arkansas

How to Get There: From US-62, follow signs to historic downtown Eureka Springs.

GPS Coordinates: 36.4062111° N, 93.7362919° W

Best Time to Visit: Spring and fall for the best weather and fewer crowds.

Pass/Permit/Fees: Free to explore.

Did You Know? Eureka Springs' entire downtown area is listed on the National Register of Historic Places.

Website: https://www.facebook.com/EurekaDowntown/

Eureka Springs Transit

Discover the charm of Eureka Springs by hopping on the Eureka Springs Transit, a convenient and scenic way to explore this historic town. These charming trolleys let you sit back and enjoy the beauty of Eureka Springs, known for its Victorian architecture and vibrant arts scene. Ride the trolley to visit local shops, galleries, and restaurants, making the most out of your adventure in this enchanting town.

Location: 137 W. Van Buren, Highway 62 Trolley Stop #1, Eureka Springs, AR 72632-3650

Closest City or Town: Eureka Springs, Arkansas

How to Get There: From Highway 62, head towards downtown Eureka Springs. Look for Trolley Stop #1 across from the Best Western Inn of the Ozarks.

GPS Coordinates: 36.3950150° N, 93.7456610° W

Best Time to Visit: Spring through fall to enjoy the best weather and scenery

Pass/Permit/Fees: Various fare options; see the website for details

Did You Know? Eureka Springs Transit offers narrated trolley tours that provide historical context and interesting stories about the area.

Website: http://www.eurekatrolley.org/

Keels Creek Winery

Indulge in the flavors of Arkansas at Keels Creek Winery, a boutique winery nestled in the rolling hills of Eureka Springs. This enchanting winery offers a serene setting to enjoy wine tastings, showcasing a range of varieties crafted from locally grown grapes. Wander through the vineyard, visit the art gallery featuring local artists, and savor the harmonious blend of fine wine and fine art.

Location: 3185 E van Buren, Eureka Springs, AR 72632-9498

Closest City or Town: Eureka Springs, Arkansas

How to Get There: From downtown Eureka Springs, take US-62 E for about 3 miles. The winery will be on your right.

GPS Coordinates: 36.3903713° N, 93.7134208° W

Best Time to Visit: Year-round, offering a cozy escape in any season

Pass/Permit/Fees: Fees for wine tastings; see the website for details

Did You Know? Keels Creek Winery specializes in producing wines from French-American hybrid and Native American grapes.

Website: http://www.keelscreek.com/

Lake Leatherwood

Embrace the great outdoors at Lake Leatherwood, a serene retreat offering a myriad of recreational activities. This stunning lake and the surrounding park provide the perfect setting for fishing, boating, hiking, and mountain biking. Paddle across the tranquil waters, hike along scenic trails, or simply enjoy a picnic amidst the natural beauty of this idyllic Arkansas destination.

Location: 532 Spring St, Eureka Springs, AR 72632-3033

Closest City or Town: Eureka Springs, Arkansas

How to Get There: From Eureka Springs, take US-62 W and follow the signs to the park entrance off Magnetic Road.

GPS Coordinates: 36.4102834° N, 93.7405335° W

Best Time to Visit: Spring through fall for the best outdoor conditions

Pass/Permit/Fees: No entrance fee; some activities may have fees

Did You Know? Lake Leatherwood covers 85 acres and is fed by one of the largest hand-cut native limestone dams in the country.

Website:
http://www.lakeleatherwoodcitypark.com/lakeleatherwoodpark.htm

Onyx Cave Park

Discover the wonders of the underground at Onyx Cave Park, one of Arkansas's oldest show caves located just outside of Eureka Springs. Take a self-guided tour through this natural marvel, marveling at the stunning formations that have developed over millennia. The cave's cool, constant temperature makes it a refreshing summer escape and a fascinating educational expedition year-round.

Location: 338 Onyx Cave Ln, Eureka Springs, AR 72632-9631

Closest City or Town: Eureka Springs, Arkansas

How to Get There: From downtown Eureka Springs, take US-62 E to Rock House Road, then follow signs to Onyx Cave Lane.

GPS Coordinates: 36.4423338° N, 93.6816961° W

Best Time to Visit: Year-round, featuring a constant cave temperature

Pass/Permit/Fees: Tour fees apply; check the website for details

Did You Know? Onyx Cave was discovered in 1893 and offers some of the most stunning calcite formations in the region.

Website:
https://www.facebook.com/profile.php?id=100057458747350

Pivot Rock and Natural Bridge

Find your sense of wonder at Pivot Rock and Natural Bridge, a captivating natural formation near Eureka Springs. This unique geological site features a towering rock that appears precariously balanced and an impressive natural bridge spanning a scenic ravine. Wander along the trails, take in the remarkable views, and perhaps enjoy a family picnic surrounded by these awe-inspiring natural structures.

Location: 1708 Pivot Rock Rd, Eureka Springs, AR 72632-9403

Closest City or Town: Eureka Springs, Arkansas

How to Get There: From downtown Eureka Springs, take Pivot Rock Road northwest for about 2 miles until you reach the destination.

GPS Coordinates: 36.4314796° N, 93.7477929° W

Best Time to Visit: Spring through fall for the best outdoor conditions

Pass/Permit/Fees: Entry fees apply; see the website for details

Did You Know? Pivot Rock is known for its unusual balancing act that defies gravity, making it a popular subject for photography.

Website: https://pivotrockpark.com/

Quicksilver Gallery

Find your sense of wonder and creativity at Quicksilver Gallery, a charming art space located in the heart of Eureka Springs, Arkansas. This eclectic gallery showcases a vibrant collection of paintings, sculptures, jewelry, and crafts from local and regional artists. Wander through the beautifully curated exhibits, and discover unique pieces that capture the essence of the Ozarks' artistic spirit.

Location: 73 Spring St, Eureka Springs, AR 72632-3147

Closest City or Town: Eureka Springs, Arkansas

How to Get There: From downtown Eureka Springs, head north on Main Street, turn right onto Spring Street, and look for the gallery near the corner.

GPS Coordinates: 36.4036498° N, 93.7371553° W

Best Time to Visit: Year-round for ever-changing exhibits.

Pass/Permit/Fees: Free to enter.

Did You Know? Quicksilver Gallery often hosts artist receptions and special events, making it a lively cultural hub in Eureka Springs.

Website: http://www.quicksilvergallery.com/

Quigley's Castle

Step into a whimsical world at Quigley's Castle, billed as Ozarks' Strangest Dwelling, located near Eureka Springs, Arkansas. Designed and handbuilt by Elise Quigley in the 1940s, this unique home is adorned with an enchanting mosaic of stones, shells, and glass. Stroll through the lush gardens filled with exotic plants, and marvel at the creativity that makes this a must-visit destination for curious minds and art lovers.

Location: 274 Quigley Castle Rd, Eureka Springs, AR 72632-9144

Closest City or Town: Eureka Springs, Arkansas

How to Get There: From downtown Eureka Springs, take US-62 W for about 4 miles, then turn left onto Quigley Castle Rd.

GPS Coordinates: 36.3461675° N, 93.7560505° W

Best Time to Visit: Spring and summer for the garden blooms.

Pass/Permit/Fees: Admission fees apply.

Did You Know? Quigley's Castle is listed on the National Register of Historic Places, a testament to its unique artistry and history.

Website: http://www.quigleyscastle.com/

St. Elizabeth's Catholic Church

Find your sense of peace and reflection at St. Elizabeth's Catholic Church, a historical gem perched on the hills of Eureka Springs, Arkansas. This charming church, built in the early 20th century, stands out for its unique entry through the bell tower design. Marvel at the beautiful stained glass windows and enjoy the serene views from the church garden.

Location: 30 Crescent Dr Historic Loop, Eureka Springs, AR 72632-3037

Closest City or Town: Eureka Springs, Arkansas

How to Get There: From downtown Eureka Springs, take Spring Street and continue onto Crescent Drive.

GPS Coordinates: 36.4076052° N, 93.7370016° W

Best Time to Visit: Year-round, with special services held during religious holidays.

Pass/Permit/Fees: Free to enter.

Did You Know? St. Elizabeth's offers one of the best panoramic views of Eureka Springs from its elevated location.

Website: https://stelizabetheureka.com/

FAIRFIELD BAY

Fairfield Bay Marina

Discover a haven for water enthusiasts at Fairfield Bay Marina, nestled along the shores of Greers Ferry Lake in Fairfield Bay, Arkansas. This full-service marina offers boat rentals, guided fishing tours, and a variety of water sports equipment for a fun-filled day on the water. Perfect for families and adventurers alike, the marina also features a charming café with stunning lakeside views.

Location: 4350 Highway 330 S, Fairfield Bay, AR 72153-5033

Closest City or Town: Fairfield Bay, Arkansas

How to Get There: From US-65, take AR-92 E towards Fairfield Bay, then follow signs to the marina on Highway 330 S.

GPS Coordinates: 35.5677903° N, 92.2982146° W

Best Time to Visit: Summer months for water activities.

Pass/Permit/Fees: Fees vary for boat rentals and tours.

Did You Know? Fairfield Bay Marina is renowned for its spectacular sunset cruises, offering breathtaking views of Greers Ferry Lake.

Website: http://visitfairfieldbay.com/marina/marina

FAYETTEVILLE

Baum Stadium

Find your sense of school spirit and athletic excitement at Baum Stadium, home to the Arkansas Razorbacks baseball team in Fayetteville, Arkansas. This state-of-the-art stadium features comfortable seating, excellent sightlines, and a lively atmosphere that make it one of the premier college baseball venues in the nation. Catch a game and cheer on the Hogs with fellow fans.

Location: 1255 S Razorback Rd, Fayetteville, AR 72701-7870

Closest City or Town: Fayetteville, Arkansas

How to Get There: From I-49, take exit 61 and follow AR-112 N to S Razorback Rd.

GPS Coordinates: 36.0498883° N, 94.1822406° W

Best Time to Visit: Spring through early summer during baseball season.

Pass/Permit/Fees: Ticket prices vary depending on the game.

Did You Know? Baum Stadium has been named the best college baseball stadium in America by Baseball America.

Website:
http://www.hogwired.com/ViewArticle.dbml?DB_OEM_ID=6100&KEY=&ATCLID=187022

Botanical Garden of the Ozarks

Find your sense of wonder at the Botanical Garden of the Ozarks, nestled in Fayetteville, Arkansas. This enchanting 44-acre haven invites visitors to explore themed gardens, beautiful walking trails, and vibrant displays of native flora. Seasonal events like butterfly releases and garden festivals make each visit unique. Don't miss the chance to relax in the Japanese Garden or marvel at the butterfly house filled with colorful, winged wonders. With year-round beauty and educational programs, it's a cornerstone of the community, offering both locals and travelers a serene escape into nature.

Location: 4703 N Crossover Rd, Fayetteville, AR 72764-9127

Closest City or Town: Fayetteville, Arkansas

How to Get There: From downtown Fayetteville, head east on AR-45 E/ Mission Blvd, turn left on Crossover Rd and continue to the garden entrance.

GPS Coordinates: 36.1365129° N, 94.1193538° W

Best Time to Visit: Spring and summer for the fullest blooms

Pass/Permit/Fees: Admission fees apply

Did You Know? The garden features a mesmerizing Butterfly House that opens in June and visitors can walk among dozens of species of native butterflies.

Website: http://www.bgozarks.org/

Clinton House Museum

Step back in time at the Clinton House Museum in Fayetteville, Arkansas, where you can explore the first home of President Bill Clinton and Secretary of State Hillary Rodham Clinton. This charming 1930s bungalow, located in a historic neighborhood, offers an intimate glimpse into the Clintons' early lives. Visitors can peruse exhibits featuring memorabilia, photographs, and personal letters that tell the story of their journey from Arkansas to the White House. The quaint garden, filled with heritage plants, adds to the charm and nostalgia of this modest yet significant home.

Location: 930 W Clinton Dr, Fayetteville, AR 72701-4912

Closest City or Town: Fayetteville, Arkansas

How to Get There: From downtown Fayetteville, head south on S School Ave, turn right on W Clinton Dr; the museum will be on the left.

GPS Coordinates: 36.0632336° N, 94.1739859° W

Best Time to Visit: Spring and fall for mild weather

Pass/Permit/Fees: Admission fees apply

Did You Know? Bill and Hillary Clinton were married in the living room of this very house in 1975.

Website: http://www.clintonhousemuseum.org/

Donald W. Reynolds Razorback Stadium

Roar with the Razorbacks at Donald W. Reynolds Razorback Stadium, the heart of Arkansas football. Located in Fayetteville, this massive venue holds over 76,000 fans and creates an electrifying atmosphere on game days. Experience the thrill as you cheer for the University of Arkansas Razorbacks, participate in tailgating events, and soak up the collegiate spirit. The stadium's state-of-the-art facilities and stunning views of the Ozarks make it a top destination for sports enthusiasts.

Location: 350 N Razorback Rd, Fayetteville, AR 72701-3954

Closest City or Town: Fayetteville, Arkansas

How to Get There: From downtown Fayetteville, head north on Razorback Rd to reach the stadium entrance.

GPS Coordinates: 36.0680503° N, 94.1789239° W

Best Time to Visit: Fall for the football season

Pass/Permit/Fees: Ticket fees apply for events

Did You Know? In 2001, the stadium underwent a $110 million renovation, including the addition of the giant video scoreboard PigScreen.

Website:
http://www.arkansasrazorbacks.com/ViewArticle.dbml?DB_OEM_ID=6100&ATCLID=187018

Lake Fayetteville

Reconnect with nature at Lake Fayetteville, a sprawling 458-acre reservoir in Fayetteville, Arkansas. This outdoor haven offers limitless recreational activities, from fishing and boating to hiking and cycling along the 5.5-mile nature trail. Birdwatchers and photographers will delight in the local wildlife and scenic views. Ideal for family outings or solo adventures, the park also features additional amenities like a disc golf course and picnic areas for a full day of fun.

Location: 1330 E Lake Fayetteville Rd, Fayetteville, AR 72764

Closest City or Town: Fayetteville, Arkansas

How to Get There: From downtown Fayetteville, take US-71B N to Lake Fayetteville Rd and follow signs to the lake entrance.

GPS Coordinates: 36.1355006° N, 94.1374468° W

Best Time to Visit: Spring through fall

Pass/Permit/Fees: Free to enter; some amenities may have fees

Did You Know? Lake Fayetteville is home to the botanical garden of the Ozarks, making it a diverse spot for both recreation and education.

Website: http://www.lakefay.com/

Square Gardens

Experience the vibrant community atmosphere at Square Gardens, located in the heart of Fayetteville, Arkansas. This beautifully landscaped square is surrounded by historic buildings, charming shops, and cozy cafes. It's a hub for local events, from the seasonal farmers' market to the festive Lights of the Ozarks display. Stroll through the lush gardens, enjoy public art installations, and soak up the unique charm of this central gathering place, making your visit to Fayetteville truly memorable.

Location: 1 W Center Street, Fayetteville, AR 72701

Closest City or Town: Fayetteville, Arkansas

How to Get There: From US-71B, head toward downtown Fayetteville, turning onto Center St to reach the square.

GPS Coordinates: 36.0622222° N, 94.1602778° W

Best Time to Visit: Spring through fall

Pass/Permit/Fees: Free to explore

Did You Know? The Fayetteville Farmers' Market has been hosted at Square Gardens since 1973.

Website: https://www.fayetteville-ar.gov/facilities/facility/details/square-gardens-57

TheatreSquared

Find your sense of creativity at TheatreSquared, an acclaimed performing arts venue located in Fayetteville, Arkansas. This dynamic theater is known for producing engaging, high-quality productions that range from classic masterpieces to contemporary premieres. Visitors can immerse themselves in the intimate atmosphere of this state-of-the-art facility, enjoying a diverse array of performances that capture the essence of human experience. Positioned in the heart of Fayetteville, TheatreSquared provides an artistic oasis for both the local community and visitors.

Location: 477 W Spring St, Fayetteville, AR 72701-5027

Closest City or Town: Fayetteville, Arkansas

How to Get There: From I-49, take exit 62 and head north on US-62/MLK Jr Blvd. Turn right onto S Block Ave, then left onto W Spring St.

GPS Coordinates: 36.0646590° N, 94.1653142° W

Best Time to Visit: Year-round, with performances varying by season

Pass/Permit/Fees: Ticket prices vary by performance; see website

Did You Know? TheatreSquared is one of the fastest-growing theater companies in the country.

Website: https://www.facebook.com/TheatreSquared/

Walton Arts Center

Immerse yourself in a world of cultural diversity at the Walton Arts Center, nestled in the vibrant Dickson Street entertainment district of Fayetteville, Arkansas. This premier arts facility hosts a myriad of performances from Broadway musicals and symphony concerts to dance and theater productions, offering something for every art lover. Its prime location fosters a lively atmosphere, making it a cornerstone of the local arts scene and a hub for entertainment and education.

Location: 495 W Dickson St, Fayetteville, AR 72701-5108

Closest City or Town: Fayetteville, Arkansas

How to Get There: From I-49, take exit 64 and follow AR-112 S towards Fayetteville. Turn left on W Dickson St.

GPS Coordinates: 36.0660020° N, 94.1648529° W

Best Time to Visit: Throughout the year, with different events each season

Pass/Permit/Fees: Pricing varies by event; see website for details

Did You Know? The Walton Arts Center was a catalyst for the revitalization of Fayetteville's downtown area.

Website: http://www.waltonartscenter.org/

Wilson Park

Relax and rejuvenate at Wilson Park, an urban oasis located in Fayetteville, Arkansas. Spanning 22.75 acres, this historic park features lush greenery, walking trails, tennis courts, playgrounds, and the beloved Castle, a whimsical structure created by local artist Frank Williams. Positioned near the University of Arkansas campus, Wilson Park offers a peaceful respite amidst nature, ideal for family picnics, morning jogs, or simply soaking in the serene environment.

Location: 675 N Park Ave, Fayetteville, AR 72701-3436

Closest City or Town: Fayetteville, Arkansas

How to Get There: From I-49, take exit 64 and drive east on AR-112 S. Continue on W Maple St to N Park Ave.

GPS Coordinates: 36.0734440° N, 94.1608522° W

Best Time to Visit: Spring through fall for the best weather

Pass/Permit/Fees: Free to enter

Did You Know? Wilson Park is home to some of Fayetteville's oldest and largest trees.

Website:
http://www.accessfayetteville.org/government/parks_and_recreation/parks/wilson_park.cfm

FIFTY SIX

Blanchard Springs Caverns

Step into the subterranean wonderland of Blanchard Springs Caverns, an awe-inspiring cave system located in the Ozark-St. Francis National Forests near Fifty Six, Arkansas. This spectacular geological marvel features guided tours through lushly decorated rooms teeming with stalactites, stalagmites, and flowstones. Exploring these vast underground chambers, you will marvel at the intricate formations sculpted by nature over millennia, making it a must-visit for adventurers and geology enthusiasts alike.

Location: 704 Blanchard Springs Rd, Fifty Six, AR 72533

Closest City or Town: Fifty Six, Arkansas

How to Get There: From US-65, take AR-14 W to AR-87 in Fifty Six, then follow signs to Blanchard Springs Rd.

GPS Coordinates: 35.9638659° N, 92.1793056° W

Best Time to Visit: Year-round, with constant cave temperatures providing a cool escape

Pass/Permit/Fees: Tour fees apply; see the website for details

Did You Know? Blanchard Springs Caverns is often referred to as the Living Crystal Chamber due to its continuously growing formations.

Website:
https://www.fs.usda.gov/detail/osfnf/specialplaces/?cid=stelprdb53 51305

FORT SMITH

Fort Smith Museum of History

Delve into the rich tapestry of Arkansas' past at the Fort Smith Museum of History, located in the heart of Fort Smith. This intriguing museum houses a wide array of artifacts spanning the region's history, from early Native American inhabitants to the bustling days of the Old West. Visitors can explore meticulously curated exhibits that feature antique fire engines, period costumes, Civil War memorabilia, and more, offering a comprehensive overview of local heritage.

Location: 320 Rogers Ave, Fort Smith, AR 72901-1937

Closest City or Town: Fort Smith, Arkansas

How to Get There: From I-540, take exit 8B and merge onto AR-22 E/Rogers Ave. Continue on Rogers Ave; the museum will be on your right.

GPS Coordinates: 35.3876140° N, 94.4283300° W

Best Time to Visit: Year-round, with special events held throughout the year

Pass/Permit/Fees: Admission fees apply; see the website for more information

Did You Know? The museum's building, constructed in 1906, is listed on the National Register of Historic Places.

Website: http://www.fortsmithmuseum.com/

Fort Smith National Cemetery

Find your sense of reverence and reflection at Fort Smith National Cemetery, a solemn and historic site located in Fort Smith, Arkansas. This beautifully maintained cemetery honors the resting places of American military veterans and their families, dating back to the Civil War. Wander among the rows of uniform white headstones, each telling a story of bravery and sacrifice. The serene landscape, stately trees, and monuments provide a peaceful setting for contemplation and remembrance.

Location: 522 Garland Avenue and South 6th Street, Fort Smith, AR 72901

Closest City or Town: Fort Smith, Arkansas

How to Get There: From I-540, take exit 8B and merge onto AR-22 E/Rogers Ave. Follow signs for Garland Avenue and South 6th Street to reach the cemetery.

GPS Coordinates: 35.3840860° N, 94.4293070° W

Best Time to Visit: Year-round, with Memorial Day and Veterans Day offering special ceremonies

Pass/Permit/Fees: Free to enter

Did You Know? Fort Smith National Cemetery is one of only a few national cemeteries where both Union and Confederate soldiers are buried.

Website: http://www.cem.va.gov/CEM/cems/nchp/ftsmith.asp

Fort Smith National Historic Site

Step back in time at the Fort Smith National Historic Site, located in Fort Smith, Arkansas. This fascinating park preserves the remnants of two frontier forts, along with the iconic federal courthouse where Judge Isaac Parker, the "Hanging Judge," held court. Visitors can explore the reconstructed gallows, the historic jail known as Hell on the Border, and interactive exhibits that tell tales from the Wild West.

Location: 301 Parker Ave, Fort Smith, AR 72901-1938

Closest City or Town: Fort Smith, Arkansas

How to Get There: From I-540, take exit 8B and merge onto AR-22 E/Rogers Ave. Turn left onto Parker Ave and follow signs to the site.

GPS Coordinates: 35.3881390° N, 94.4299163° W

Best Time to Visit: Year-round; spring and fall offer pleasant weather

Pass/Permit/Fees: Entry fees apply for adults; discounts for seniors and children

Did You Know? Fort Smith was a significant frontier outpost established in 1817 to maintain peace between Native American tribes.

Website: http://www.nps.gov/fosm/index.htm

Miss Laura's Visitor Center

Discover the charming history of Fort Smith at Miss Laura's Visitor Center, a unique and colorful destination located in Fort Smith, Arkansas. Housed in a beautifully restored 1903 bordello, this visitor center offers a quirky yet educational insight into the city's past. Join a guided tour to learn about the colorful life of Miss Laura and her establishment's role in the Wild West.

Location: 2 N B St, Fort Smith, AR 72901-1126

Closest City or Town: Fort Smith, Arkansas

How to Get There: From I-540, take exit 8B and merge onto AR-22 E/Rogers Ave. Turn left onto N B St.

GPS Coordinates: 35.3920583° N, 94.4291594° W

Best Time to Visit: Year-round, with spring and fall offering the best weather for strolling around

Pass/Permit/Fees: Free to enter; donations accepted

Did You Know? Miss Laura's is the only former bordello on the National Register of Historic Places.

Website: http://www.misslaurasvc.com/

GARFIELD

Pea Ridge National Military Park

Immerse yourself in Civil War history at Pea Ridge National Military Park, located in Garfield, Arkansas. This 4,300-acre park preserves the site of the pivotal Battle of Pea Ridge, which played a crucial role in the Union's victory in the Western Theater. Explore the extensive trails, visit the museum exhibits, and stand on the battlefield where history was made.

Location: 15930 E Highway 62, Garfield, AR 72732-9532

Closest City or Town: Garfield, Arkansas

How to Get There: From US-62 E, drive toward Garfield and follow signs to the park entrance.

GPS Coordinates: 36.4433394° N, 94.0266101° W

Best Time to Visit: Spring and fall for pleasant weather and reenactments

Pass/Permit/Fees: Entrance fees apply

Did You Know? Pea Ridge is one of the most well-preserved Civil War battlefields, offering a glimpse into 1862 military strategy and life.

Website: http://www.nps.gov/peri/index.htm

GENTRY

Wild Wilderness Drive-Through Safari

Set out on a wild adventure at the Wild Wilderness Drive-Through Safari in Gentry, Arkansas. This family-friendly attraction allows you to explore a sprawling 400-acre wildlife park from the comfort of your car. Encounter a variety of exotic animals, including zebras, camels, and lions, in a naturalistic setting. The park also offers a petting zoo, pony rides, and a walk-through area for up-close experiences.

Location: 20923 Safari Rd, Gentry, AR 72734-8922

Closest City or Town: Gentry, Arkansas

How to Get There: From US-412, head west on AR-59 N towards Gentry. Turn left onto Safari Road and follow signs to the entrance.

GPS Coordinates: 36.2970345° N, 94.4960676° W

Best Time to Visit: Spring through fall for the best weather and animal activity

Pass/Permit/Fees: Admission fees apply

Did You Know? Wild Wilderness is home to over 85 different species of animals, making it a unique and educational outing for all ages.

Website: http://www.gentryzoo.com/

GREENBRIER

Woolly Hollow State Park

Embrace the tranquility and natural beauty at Woolly Hollow State Park, a serene getaway located in Greenbrier, Arkansas. This picturesque park invites visitors to explore its lush woodlands, hike along scenic trails, and enjoy the crystal-clear waters of Lake Bennett. Nestled in the Ozark foothills, Woolly Hollow offers a peaceful retreat with activities including fishing, swimming, picnicking, and camping. The park's unique feature is its historic Woolly Cabin, giving a glimpse into pioneer life, surrounded by a beautiful landscape perfect for exploration and relaxation.

Location: 82 Woolly Hollow Rd, Greenbrier, AR 72058-9788

Closest City or Town: Greenbrier, Arkansas

How to Get There: From US-65, head east on AR-285, and follow the signs to Woolly Hollow Rd.

GPS Coordinates: 35.2887434° N, 92.2869995° W

Best Time to Visit: Spring and summer for outdoor activities

Pass/Permit/Fees: Entrance fees vary; visit the website for details.

Did You Know? Lake Bennett was constructed in the 1930s by the Civilian Conservation Corps.

Website: http://www.arkansasstateparks.com/woollyhollow/

HARRISON

Triple Falls

Experience the majestic beauty of Triple Falls, a breathtaking three-tiered waterfall located in the heart of the Ozarks. Also known as Twin Falls, this natural wonder offers a tranquil escape perfect for nature lovers.

Found in the Buffalo National River area near Harrison, Arkansas, Triple Falls is accessible via a short hike through lush greenery, leading to the awe-inspiring sight of water cascading from three distinct ledges. This picturesque spot is ideal for photography, picnicking, and simply basking in the serene surroundings.

Highlighting its unique aspect, Triple Falls flows year-round, making it a must-visit regardless of the season.

Location: 3P4R+JX Harrison, Arkansas

Closest City or Town: Harrison, Arkansas

How to Get There: From Harrison, drive south on Highway 7 to Jasper. Head west on Arkansas 74, then follow signs to Camp Orr. The trailhead begins near the camp.

GPS Coordinates: 36.0565625° N, 93.2575625° W

Best Time to Visit: Spring for the most powerful flow

Pass/Permit/Fees: Free to visit

Did You Know? The falls are often referred to as Twin Falls due to a unique rock formation splitting the flow of water.

Website: https://www.dupontforest.com/explore/triple-falls/

HEBER SPRINGS

Greers Ferry Lake

Discover endless opportunities for fun and relaxation at Greers Ferry Lake, a pristine reservoir situated in Heber Springs, Arkansas. Renowned for its clear waters, this lake offers a paradise for outdoor enthusiasts.

Nestled in the foothills of the Ozark Mountains, Greers Ferry Lake boasts over 40,000 acres perfect for water activities like boating, fishing, and swimming. Visitors can also explore the surrounding lush forests and trails.

The lake's unique feature is the captivating Sand Island, a sandy oasis perfect for beach volleyball and sunbathing.

Location: GVJ5+47 Heber Springs, Arkansas

Closest City or Town: Heber Springs, Arkansas

How to Get There: Located off AR-25; follow signs from the main road to the lake access points.

GPS Coordinates: 35.5303632° N, 92.1418281° W

Best Time to Visit: Summer months for water activities

Pass/Permit/Fees: Free access; certain amenities may have fees

Did You Know? Greers Ferry Lake was dedicated by President John F. Kennedy in 1963.

Website: https://www.recreation.gov/camping/gateways/537

HOPE

President William Jefferson Clinton Birthplace Home

Explore the early beginnings of a president at the President William Jefferson Clinton Birthplace Home, located in Hope, Arkansas. This quaint home offers a fascinating look into the early life of Bill Clinton, highlighting his humble roots and the community that shaped him. Located in a charming neighborhood, visitors can tour the restored house, view personal artifacts, and learn about Clinton's rise to the White House. The serene surroundings provide a reflective backdrop, making it an educational and inspiring stop.

Location: 117 S Hervey St, Hope, AR 71801-4208

Closest City or Town: Hope, Arkansas

How to Get There: Accessible via I-30, take the exit toward Hope and follow the signs to S Hervey St.

GPS Coordinates: 33.6675835° N, 93.5964186° W

Best Time to Visit: Spring and fall for mild weather

Pass/Permit/Fees: Free to enter

Did You Know? Bill Clinton was born William Jefferson Blythe III and took his stepfather's surname at age 15.

Website: http://www.nps.gov/

HOT SPRINGS

Anthony Chapel

Find your sense of peace and elegance at Anthony Chapel, a stunning architectural marvel in Hot Springs, Arkansas. Nestled within the Garvan Woodland Gardens, this breathtaking chapel features floor-to-ceiling glass walls and soaring timber beams, creating a serene sanctuary harmoniously blended with nature. Visitors can revel in the peaceful ambiance, attend a wedding, or simply enjoy a moment of reflection amidst the natural beauty. The chapel's unique design provides an unforgettable experience, making it a perfect spot for unforgettable ceremonies and quiet contemplation.

Location: 550 Arkridge Rd, Hot Springs, AR 71913-8729

Closest City or Town: Hot Springs, Arkansas

How to Get There: From downtown Hot Springs, take Highway 70 West and follow signs for Arkridge Road.

GPS Coordinates: 34.4355043° N, 93.0437198° W

Best Time to Visit: Spring and fall for vibrant foliage and comfortable weather

Pass/Permit/Fees: Admission fees apply; check the website for details.

Did You Know? Anthony Chapel is often booked years in advance for weddings due to its stunning architecture and natural setting.

Website: https://www.garvangardens.org/weddings/anthony-chapel/

Arkansas Alligator Farm & Petting Zoo

Dive into an exciting adventure at the Arkansas Alligator Farm & Petting Zoo, located in the historic town of Hot Springs. This unique farm offers an up-close and personal experience with alligators, emus, and a variety of friendly farm animals. Situated just minutes from downtown, visitors can watch alligator feedings, hold baby alligators, and explore the petting zoo. The farm's star attraction is its large collection of alligators, providing thrilling demonstrations that captivate both young and old alike.

Location: 847 Whittington Ave, Hot Springs, AR 71901-3318

Closest City or Town: Hot Springs, Arkansas

How to Get There: From downtown Hot Springs, head northwest on Whittington Avenue.

GPS Coordinates: 34.5151290° N, 93.0725021° W

Best Time to Visit: Spring and summer for optimal animal activity

Pass/Permit/Fees: Admission fees apply; see the website for details.

Did You Know? The Arkansas Alligator Farm has been a family-owned attraction since 1902, making it one of the oldest in the state.

Website: https://alligatorfarmzoo.com/

Buckstaff Bathhouse

Experience the rejuvenating legacy of Buckstaff Bathhouse, an iconic destination in Hot Springs National Park, Arkansas. Since 1912, this historic facility has been offering therapeutic baths and massages using the park's famous thermal waters. Located on Bathhouse Row, guests can indulge in the traditional bath treatments, enjoy steam cabinets, and relax with a full-body massage. Buckstaff's unique feature is its adherence to traditional techniques, providing an authentic and nostalgic spa experience steeped in history.

Location: 509 Central Ave, Hot Springs, AR 71901-3596

Closest City or Town: Hot Springs, Arkansas

How to Get There: From Highway 70, take Central Avenue towards downtown Hot Springs.

GPS Coordinates: 34.5124015° N, 93.0535376° W

Best Time to Visit: Year-round, with peak seasons in spring and fall

Pass/Permit/Fees: Fees vary depending on treatments; visit the website for details.

Did You Know? Buckstaff Bathhouse is the only facility on Bathhouse Row that has operated continuously since the day it opened.

Website: http://www.buckstaffbaths.com/

Funtrackers Family Fun Park

Find your sense of adventure and excitement at Funtrackers Family Fun Park in Hot Springs, Arkansas. This action-packed destination offers a variety of thrilling activities that are sure to delight visitors of all ages. From high-speed go-kart racing and mini-golf to bumper boats and an arcade, Funtrackers provides endless family-friendly entertainment. The park's unique appeal lies in its combination of attractions that promise fun for everyone, whether you're looking to compete or simply unwind.

Location: 2614 Albert Pike Rd, Hot Springs, AR 71913-4513

Closest City or Town: Hot Springs, Arkansas

How to Get There: Take the US-70 W/Albert Pike Rd from downtown Hot Springs; the park is located on the right side.

GPS Coordinates: 34.4948821° N, 93.1176807° W

Best Time to Visit: Spring through fall for optimal weather conditions

Pass/Permit/Fees: Admission fees apply for each attraction

Did You Know? Funtrackers features a challenging 18-hole mini-golf course that offers fun obstacles and scenic views.

Website: http://www.funtrackersfamilypark.com/

Gangster Museum of America

Step into the intriguing world of the 1920s and 1930s at the Gangster Museum of America, located in Hot Springs, Arkansas. This fascinating museum takes you back to an era when Hot Springs was a favorite retreat for America's most notorious gangsters. Through engaging exhibits, artifacts, and restored rooms, learn about the city's colorful past, its ties to infamous figures like Al Capone, and its unique blend of vice and glamour that once made it a hotbed for illegal activities.

Location: 510 Central Ave, Hot Springs, AR 71901-3597

Closest City or Town: Hot Springs, Arkansas

How to Get There: Take Central Ave/AR-7 from the city center, and the museum will be on your left.

GPS Coordinates: 34.5123029° N, 93.0544025° W

Best Time to Visit: Year-round for immersive historical experiences

Pass/Permit/Fees: Entrance fees apply

Did You Know? The museum offers guided tours that provide deeper insights into the stories and secrets of the gangsters who frequented the area.

Website: http://www.tgmoa.com/

Grand Promenade

Discover the elegance and beauty of the Grand Promenade, a scenic walkway that showcases the charm of Hot Springs National Park. This gracefully designed path provides spectacular views of historic downtown Hot Springs, lush landscapes, and natural springs. Ideal for a leisurely stroll, the Grand Promenade links to several trails within the park, inviting visitors to explore its rich natural and cultural history.

Location: 369 Central Ave, Hot Springs, AR 71901

Closest City or Town: Hot Springs, Arkansas

How to Get There: Access the promenade from Central Avenue in downtown Hot Springs.

GPS Coordinates: 34.5138641° N, 93.0529983° W

Best Time to Visit: Spring and fall for pleasant weather and beautiful scenery

Pass/Permit/Fees: Free to enter

Did You Know? The Grand Promenade was constructed in the 1930s as part of a major development project to enhance the park's accessibility and beauty.

Website: https://www.nps.gov/places/grand-promenade.htm

Lake Catherine State Park

Immerse yourself in the natural beauty and outdoor adventures at Lake Catherine State Park in Hot Springs, Arkansas. This picturesque park offers a variety of recreational activities, including hiking, camping, boating, and fishing, all centered around the serene Lake Catherine. Enjoy scenic trails like the Falls Branch Trail, which leads to a stunning waterfall, or relax by the water's edge. The campgrounds and cabins provide the perfect settings for an overnight getaway amidst nature.

Location: 1200 Catherine Park Rd, Hot Springs, AR 71913-8716

Closest City or Town: Hot Springs, Arkansas

How to Get There: From Hot Springs, take AR-171 S and follow signs to Lake Catherine State Park.

GPS Coordinates: 34.4287378° N, 92.9226486° W

Best Time to Visit: Spring through fall for the best outdoor activities

Pass/Permit/Fees: Entrance to the park is free; fees apply for camping and cabin rentals

Did You Know? Lake Catherine State Park is home to one of the state's oldest CCC-built cabins, which dates back to the 1930s.

Website: https://en.wikipedia.org/wiki/Lake_Catherine_State_Park

Magic Springs Theme and Water Park

Get ready for a day packed with thrills and laughter at Magic Springs Theme and Water Park in Hot Springs, Arkansas. This exhilarating park offers visitors an exciting combination of roller coasters, water rides, and family-friendly attractions. Whether you want to plunge down a water slide, brave a towering coaster, or enjoy live entertainment, Magic Springs has something for everyone.

Location: 1701 E Grand Ave, Hot Springs, AR 71901-4802

Closest City or Town: Hot Springs, Arkansas

How to Get There: Head east on Grand Ave/US-70 E from downtown Hot Springs until you reach the park entrance.

GPS Coordinates: 34.5198944° N, 93.0180794° W

Best Time to Visit: Summer for the full theme park and water park experience

Pass/Permit/Fees: Admission fees apply; season passes available

Did You Know? Magic Springs hosts a summer concert series featuring performances by popular artists and bands.

Website: http://www.magicsprings.com/

Mid-America Science Museum

Embark on an exciting journey of discovery at the Mid-America Science Museum in Hot Springs, Arkansas. This interactive museum invites visitors to explore the wonders of science through hands-on exhibits, a state-of-the-art planetarium, and thrilling outdoor adventures. Located amidst the scenic Ouachita Mountains, the museum offers a unique blend of education and entertainment. From exploring the complexities of robotics to walking through the forest canopy on a suspended bridge, every corner of this museum sparks curiosity and imagination.

Location: 500 Mid America Blvd, Hot Springs, AR 71913-8412

Closest City or Town: Hot Springs, Arkansas

How to Get There: From Highway 70, take the exit signposted Mid-America Blvd; the museum is well-signposted from there.

GPS Coordinates: 34.5157530° N, 93.1165593° W

Best Time to Visit: Year-round for various seasonal exhibits and programs

Pass/Permit/Fees: Admission fees apply; see website for ticket prices

Did You Know? The Mid-America Science Museum is home to the Arkansas Underwater Gallery, a 20,000-gallon aquarium filled with local aquatic species.

Website: http://www.midamericamuseum.org/

Mountain Valley Spring Water Visitor Center & Museum

Dive into the fascinating history of America's premier spring water at the Mountain Valley Spring Water Visitor Center & Museum, located in the heart of Hot Springs. Tour the historic bottling facility, learn about the natural spring's rich heritage, and sample the crisp, refreshing water right from its source. Nestled on Central Avenue, this museum showcases the brand's storied past and its role in the health and wellness industry.

Location: 150 Central Ave, Hot Springs, AR 71901-3528

Closest City or Town: Hot Springs, Arkansas

How to Get There: From Central Avenue, the Visitor Center is prominently located near the historic Bathhouse Row.

GPS Coordinates: 34.5175913° N, 93.0549921° W

Best Time to Visit: Year-round for the comprehensive visitor experience **Pass/Permit/Fees:** Free to enter

Did You Know? Mountain Valley Spring Water has been a favored brand of several U.S. Presidents, including John F. Kennedy and Dwight Eisenhower.

Website: http://www.mountainvalleyspring.com/mountain-valley-visitors-center.aspx

Pirate's Cove Adventure Golf

Set sail on a mini-golf adventure at Pirate's Cove Adventure Golf in Hot Springs, Arkansas. Designed with an exciting pirate theme, this 18-hole course features waterfalls, footbridges, and caves to navigate. Whether you're a seasoned mini-golf enthusiast or just looking for fun, this pirate escapade promises excitement for all ages amidst beautifully landscaped surroundings.

Location: 4612 Central Ave, Hot Springs, AR 71913-7111

Closest City or Town: Hot Springs, Arkansas

How to Get There: Located along Central Avenue, the course is easily accessible from downtown Hot Springs.

GPS Coordinates: 34.4484030° N, 93.0869304° W

Best Time to Visit: Spring through fall for the best outdoor conditions

Pass/Permit/Fees: Admission fees apply

Did You Know? Pirate's Cove Adventure Golf has been voted the best mini-golf course in America by the Miniature Golf Association.

Website: http://www.piratescove.net/location/2

Superior Bathhouse Brewery and Distillery

Discover a unique blend of history and craft brewing at the Superior Bathhouse Brewery and Distillery, located on Central Avenue in Hot Springs. As the first brewery and distillery inside a U.S. National Park and the only one in the world using thermal spring water in its brewing process, Superior offers an unparalleled tasting experience. Enjoy their innovative beers and spirits, paired with delicious bites, all while soaking in the historic ambiance of this former bathhouse.

Location: 329 Central Ave, Hot Springs, AR 71901-3525

Closest City or Town: Hot Springs, Arkansas

How to Get There: Situated on Bathhouse Row, the brewery is a central feature of downtown Hot Springs.

GPS Coordinates: 34.5148695° N, 93.0533553° W

Best Time to Visit: Year-round

Pass/Permit/Fees: Free to enter; fees for tastings and tours

Did You Know? Superior Bathhouse Brewery is the only brewery in the world that uses thermal spring water sourced directly from Hot Springs National Park in its brewing process.

Website: http://www.superiorbathhouse.com/

Thai-Me Spa

Pamper yourself with a luxurious escape at Thai-Me Spa, a premier wellness destination located in Hot Springs. Offering a soothing array of treatments, including Thai massages, facials, and body wraps, the spa ensures a rejuvenating experience. Set against the backdrop of the tranquil Ouachita Mountains, this spa promises relaxation and renewal in the heart of nature.

Location: 328 Central Ave, Hot Springs, AR 71901

Closest City or Town: Hot Springs, Arkansas

How to Get There: Located on Central Avenue in downtown Hot Springs, Thai-Me Spa is easily accessible.

GPS Coordinates: 34.5149834° N, 93.0538140° W

Best Time to Visit: Year-round

Pass/Permit/Fees: Fees vary by service; see website for details

Did You Know? Thai-Me Spa has won multiple awards for its exceptional service, making it one of the top-rated spas in Hot Springs.

Website:
https://thaime.com/?fbclid=IwZXh0bgNhZW0CMTAAAR2iuBV9Gf-Q0milu3psqox8eB1e7q27ClqmCZY54DyDKVnNIFQfLJe1cM_aem_Ae Fp1YLaNNIR6pYPk7poghuiXwOyqi6hVEHET8726TzgfAoeNAlhVKXdkTi5 11gqWeX7Dc-pmXVPHd8sy_EvtK8#

The Galaxy Connection

Step into a universe of imagination and wonder at The Galaxy Connection, a unique museum and gift shop in Hot Springs, Arkansas. Dedicated to the magic of science fiction, this destination is a haven for Star Wars and superhero fans, offering an immersive experience with life-sized characters, movie props, and collectibles. Located on Ouachita Avenue, visitors can explore displays filled with nostalgia, engage in interactive exhibits, and even dress up as their favorite characters. Highlighting its interactive approach, The Galaxy Connection lets fans of all ages delve into their favorite galaxies far, far away.

Location: 536 Ouachita Ave, Hot Springs, AR 71901-5331

Closest City or Town: Hot Springs, Arkansas

How to Get There: From downtown Hot Springs, head west on Central Avenue, turn left on Ouachita Avenue. The museum will be on the right.

GPS Coordinates: 34.5046697° N, 93.0600999° W

Best Time to Visit: Year-round, offering indoor exhibits suitable for any weather.

Pass/Permit/Fees: Entrance fees apply; check the website for details.

Did You Know? The Galaxy Connection houses one of the largest private collections of Star Wars memorabilia in the area.

Website: http://www.thegalaxyconnection.com/

Tiny Town

Unleash your inner child at Tiny Town, a whimsical miniature village in Hot Springs that has been delighting visitors for decades. This charming attraction features meticulously crafted tiny buildings, vehicles, and people, all created by hand to bring a magical world to life.

Nestled on Whittington Avenue, Tiny Town offers a nostalgic journey through a variety of scenes, from bustling cityscapes to serene countryside settings. Visitors can marvel at the intricate details and even operate some of the moving parts. The unique feature of Tiny Town is its interactive elements, allowing guests to control miniature trains and other animations.

Location: 374 Whittington Ave, Hot Springs, AR 71901-3402

Closest City or Town: Hot Springs, Arkansas

How to Get There: From downtown Hot Springs, head northwest on Central Ave. Turn left onto Whittington Ave; Tiny Town will be on your left.

GPS Coordinates: 34.5168000° N, 93.0624000° W

Best Time to Visit: Year-round, ideal for indoor fun.

Pass/Permit/Fees: Entrance fees apply; see the website for details.

Did You Know? Tiny Town started as a family's hobby and has grown into a beloved tourist attraction, captivating visitors for over 50 years.

Website: http://www.tinytowntrains.com/

JASPER

Arkansas Grand Canyon

Discover the breathtaking beauty of the Arkansas Grand Canyon, a stunning vista that offers panoramic views of the lush Ozark Mountains. Located along scenic Highway 7 near Jasper, this overlook is renowned for its sweeping landscapes and vibrant foliage, especially during the fall.

Visitors can enjoy the view from the overlook, hike nearby trails, or simply soak in the serene atmosphere. The unique feature of this destination is its elevation, providing an unparalleled vantage point to admire the natural beauty of the region. It's a perfect spot for photography, picnicking, and experiencing the grandeur of the Ozarks.

Location: Highway 7, Jasper, AR 72641

Closest City or Town: Jasper, Arkansas

How to Get There: Drive north on Highway 7 from downtown Jasper; the overlook is just a short drive away.

GPS Coordinates: 35.9451607° N, 93.1629303° W

Best Time to Visit: Fall for stunning foliage, spring for blooming wildflowers.

Pass/Permit/Fees: Free to visit.

Did You Know? The Arkansas Grand Canyon provides an elevation drop of over 1,300 feet, making for spectacular and expansive scenic views.

Website: http://www.quiltingpathways.com/arkansas/scenic7.html

JERSEY

Moro Bay State Park

Experience the tranquil beauty of Moro Bay State Park, a serene escape located at the confluence of Moro Bay and Raymond Lake. This hidden gem offers a variety of outdoor activities, from boating and fishing to hiking and wildlife watching.

Nestled in Jersey, the park features scenic water views, well-maintained trails, and comfortable cabins for an overnight stay. The unique feature of Moro Bay State Park is its waterfront setting, providing endless opportunities for water-based recreation and relaxation. It's an ideal destination for a peaceful retreat into nature.

Location: 6071 Hwy 600 S, Jersey, AR 71651

Closest City or Town: Jersey, Arkansas

How to Get There: From US-278, take Highway 600 south until you reach the park entrance.

GPS Coordinates: 33.3007433° N, 92.3496204° W

Best Time to Visit: Spring and summer for outdoor activities.

Pass/Permit/Fees: Fees vary; visit the website for details.

Did You Know? Moro Bay State Park is situated at the confluence of Moro Creek and Raymond Lake with the Ouachita River, ideal for fishing enthusiasts.

Website: http://arkansasstateparks.com/morobay

JONESBORO

Craighead Forest Park

Immerse yourself in the natural beauty and recreational opportunities at Craighead Forest Park, a beloved destination in Jonesboro. This expansive park offers something for everyone, from scenic trails and fishing spots to playgrounds and picnic areas.

Located on the outskirts of Jonesboro, Craighead Forest Park features a picturesque lake, diverse wildlife, and well-maintained facilities. Visitors can hike, bike, fish, or simply relax in the serene environment. The unique feature of this park is its accessibility and variety of activities, making it a perfect spot for family outings and nature enthusiasts.

Location: 4910 S Culberhouse Rd, Jonesboro, AR 72404-8820

Closest City or Town: Jonesboro, Arkansas

How to Get There: From downtown Jonesboro, take South Caraway Road, turn right onto South Culberhouse Road, and follow signs to the park entrance.

GPS Coordinates: 35.7770045° N, 90.7141042° W

Best Time to Visit: Spring through fall for optimal weather conditions.

Pass/Permit/Fees: Free to enter; certain amenities may have fees.

Did You Know? Craighead Forest Park was established in 1937 as a federal Works Progress Administration project, creating a lasting community treasure.

Website: http://www.jonesboro.org/parks/parks/craighead.html

Forrest L Wood Crowley's Ridge Nature Center

Find your sense of adventure and discovery at Forrest L Wood Crowley's Ridge Nature Center in Jonesboro, Arkansas. This state-of-the-art facility offers an immersive experience into the unique ecology and geology of Crowley's Ridge, a rare landform in the Mississippi Alluvial Plain. Located within a lush 160-acre site, the center

ARKANSAS BUCKET LIST

features interactive exhibits, a film theater, and educational programs. Explore the winding trails, observe wildlife, or enjoy a serene picnic amidst the natural beauty. The center's highlight is the opportunity to learn about the region's distinct environment and conservation efforts.

Location: 600 E Lawson Rd, Jonesboro, AR 72404-8897

Closest City or Town: Jonesboro, Arkansas

How to Get There: From downtown Jonesboro, take US-63 S to AR-1 S. Turn right onto E Lawson Rd and follow signs to the nature center.

GPS Coordinates: 35.7668705° N, 90.7040172° W

Best Time to Visit: Spring and fall for pleasant weather and active wildlife

Pass/Permit/Fees: Free to enter

Did You Know? Crowley's Ridge is an ancient geologic formation that rises up to 200 feet above the surrounding delta.

Website: http://www.crowleysridge.org/

KINGSTON

Hawksbill Crag

Unleash your adventurous spirit at Hawksbill Crag, also known as Whitaker Point, one of Arkansas' most iconic hiking destinations. The breathtaking crag juts out from a cliffside, offering panoramic views that are a photographer's dream.

Situated in the Ozark National Forest, this rock formation is renowned for its stunning beauty, particularly during the fall when the foliage creates a brilliant tapestry of colors. The hike to Hawksbill Crag can be challenging, but the vistas along the way make it worthwhile.

Highlighting its unique outlook, Hawksbill Crag provides the perfect perch for sunrise and sunset views.

Location: VHR5+9R Kingston, Arkansas

Closest City or Town: Kingston, Arkansas

How to Get There: From Kingston, take AR-21 N and follow signs to the trailhead parking area.

GPS Coordinates: 35.8909375° N, 93.4404375° W

Best Time to Visit: Fall for stunning foliage views

Pass/Permit/Fees: No entrance fee

Did You Know? Hawksbill Crag has been featured in several films and advertisements due to its dramatic scenery.

Website:
https://www.fs.usda.gov/recarea/osfnf/recarea/?recid=75155

Lost Valley Trail

Embark on a serene journey through nature on the Lost Valley Trail, a scenic treasure within the Buffalo National River area. This trail promises captivating landscapes and serene surroundings perfect for a day of exploration.

Beginning near the Boxley Valley, the trail winds through lush forests, alongside a creek, and eventually leads to the Eden Falls Cave. Hikers can marvel at the cascading waterfalls and explore the cave with a flashlight in hand for an unforgettable experience.

The stunning Eden Falls make this trail's unique feature, offering a peaceful oasis within the thick forest.

Location: 2J6G+35 Kingston, Arkansas

Closest City or Town: Kingston, Arkansas

How to Get There: From Kingston, take Highway 21 South towards Boxley. Turn onto Highway 43 and follow signs to the Lost Valley Trailhead.

GPS Coordinates: 36.0100982° N, 93.3737226° W

Best Time to Visit: Spring for waterfall fullness

Pass/Permit/Fees: Free to hike

Did You Know? The trail includes a natural bridge and a waterfall cave that can be explored.

Website: http://www.nps.gov/buff/index.htm

KIRBY

Daisy State Park

Discover the tranquility and scenic wonders of Daisy State Park, nestled alongside beautiful Lake Greeson in Kirby, Arkansas. This picturesque park offers a myriad of outdoor activities, from boating and fishing on the serene waters to hiking and birdwatching along the lush trails. Located in the foothills of the Ouachita Mountains, the park is a true paradise for nature enthusiasts. Camp under the stars, explore the rugged landscape, or simply relax by the water's edge. The park's unique feature is its perfect blend of mountainous terrain and sparkling lake views.

Location: 103 E Park, Kirby, AR 71950-9061

Closest City or Town: Kirby, Arkansas

How to Get There: From US-70, take AR-27 S to AR-182 W, and follow signs to the park entrance.

GPS Coordinates: 34.2336662° N, 93.7404560° W

Best Time to Visit: Spring and summer for the best outdoor activities

Pass/Permit/Fees: Entrance fees may apply; check the website for details

Did You Know? Daisy State Park is known for its excellent fishing opportunities, particularly for bass and crappie.

Website: http://www.arkansasstateparks.com/daisy/

LITTLE ROCK

Arkansas Arts Center

Immerse yourself in the world of art and culture at the Arkansas Arts Center, located in the historic MacArthur Park in Little Rock. This premier arts institution houses an impressive collection of drawings, contemporary crafts, and sculptures. Beyond its galleries, the center boasts a vibrant calendar of performances, workshops, and educational programs, making it a cultural hub for artists and art enthusiasts alike. Stroll through the beautifully curated exhibits, attend a compelling theater production, or participate in an art class. The center's standout feature is its commitment to fostering creativity and providing a space where art thrives.

Location: 501 E 9th St, Little Rock, AR 72202-3952

Closest City or Town: Little Rock, Arkansas

How to Get There: From I-630, take Exit 2A and head east on 9th St; the center is located within MacArthur Park.

GPS Coordinates: 34.7380757° N, 92.2660985° W

Best Time to Visit: Year-round, with exhibitions and events throughout the year

Pass/Permit/Fees: Free to explore; some events may have fees

Did You Know? The Arkansas Arts Center's drawings collection is one of the most comprehensive in the country.

Website: http://www.arkansasartscenter.org/

Arkansas State Capitol

Step into the heart of Arkansas's government at the Arkansas State Capitol, a grand building located in Little Rock. This awe-inspiring structure, completed in 1915, stands as a symbol of the state's history and democracy. Visitors can explore the beautiful marble halls, view historic exhibits, and even witness legislative sessions. The Capitol grounds include several statues and memorials, creating a historical journey through Arkansas's storied past. The unique feature of this destination is its striking architecture, modeled after the U.S. Capitol, complete with a stunning dome that provides panoramic views of the city.

Location: Woodlane & Capitol Avenue, Little Rock, AR 72201

Closest City or Town: Little Rock, Arkansas

How to Get There: From I-630, take Exit 1A towards Woodlane Ave and follow signs to the Capitol.

GPS Coordinates: 34.7469598° N, 92.2890500° W

Best Time to Visit: Year-round, with special tours available when the legislature is not in session

Pass/Permit/Fees: Free to enter and tour

Did You Know? The Arkansas State Capitol's front doors are made of bronze and are 10 feet tall.

Website:
http://www.sos.arkansas.gov/stateCapitolInfo/Pages/stateCapitolTour.aspx

Big Dam Bridge

Explore the longest pedestrian and bicycle bridge in North America at the iconic Big Dam Bridge in Little Rock, Arkansas. Spanning over 4,200 feet across the Arkansas River, the bridge offers stunning views and a unique way to experience the natural beauty of the area. Whether you're biking, walking, or jogging, the bridge provides a perfect route for outdoor activities. It connects over 15 miles of scenic trails and is a key highlight of the Arkansas River Trail System. Experience the breathtaking sunsets or enjoy a peaceful walk with panoramic river vistas.

Location: 7700 Rebsamen Park Rd, Little Rock, AR 72207-1616

Closest City or Town: Little Rock, Arkansas

How to Get There: From I-430, take Exit 9 and follow signs to Rebsamen Park Rd.

GPS Coordinates: 34.7902196° N, 92.3583475° W

Best Time to Visit: Spring and fall for comfortable weather

Pass/Permit/Fees: Free to access

Did You Know? The Big Dam Bridge lights up at night, creating a vibrant display over the Arkansas River.

Website: http://www.littlerock.com/little-rock-destinations/big-dam-bridge

Esse Purse Museum & Store

Unlock a world of fashion and history at the Esse Purse Museum & Store in Little Rock, Arkansas. This unique museum delves into the evolving roles of women through the lens of their handbags and accessories from the 1900s to the present day. Located in the heart of SoMa (South Main), the museum not only showcases dazzling displays of vintage purses but also provides a captivating glimpse into women's social history and fashion trends over the decades. Visitors can wander through beautifully curated exhibits, shop for unique gifts, and truly appreciate the art and storytelling behind each purse.

Location: 1510 Main St, Little Rock, AR 72202-5038

Closest City or Town: Little Rock, Arkansas

How to Get There: Take I-630 to the Main St exit and head south. The museum is situated on your right in the SoMa district.

GPS Coordinates: 34.7339829° N, 92.2733658° W

Best Time to Visit: Year-round for a continuous changing of exhibits

Pass/Permit/Fees: Admission fees apply; check the website for details.

Did You Know? Esse Purse Museum is one of only three purse museums in the world.

Website: http://essepursemuseum.com/

H. U. Lee International Gate and Garden

Discover a serene corner of international culture at the H. U. Lee International Gate and Garden in Little Rock, Arkansas. This exquisite garden stands as a symbol of friendship and cultural exchange between Arkansas and South Korea. Nestled in downtown Little Rock, it's adorned with traditional Korean gates, stone pagodas, and beautiful landscaping, providing a peaceful retreat amidst the hustle and bustle. Explore the intricate designs, enjoy the tranquility of the reflective pool, and immerse yourself in the rich cultural heritage that the garden represents.

Location: 7 Statehouse Plz, Little Rock, AR 72201-1436

Closest City or Town: Little Rock, Arkansas

How to Get There: Drive downtown via I-630, exit onto Broadway Street, turn right onto W. Markham St, and then left onto Statehouse Plaza.

GPS Coordinates: 34.7484789° N, 92.2694331° W

Best Time to Visit: Spring and fall for the most colorful views

Pass/Permit/Fees: Free to enter

Did You Know? The gate and garden commemorate Grand Master H.U. Lee, the founder of the American Taekwondo Association.

Website:
http://www.arkansas.com/attractions/detail.aspx?id=93007&r=Central&city=..

Historic Arkansas Museum

Dive into the captivating history of Arkansas at the Historic Arkansas Museum located in Little Rock. This premier institution preserves and celebrates the state's rich cultural heritage through interactive exhibits, period buildings, and engaging programs. Situated in the Quapaw Quarter, the museum offers a deep dive into the frontier history with meticulously restored historic houses and a stunning collection of decorative arts. Walk through galleries that tell the stories of Arkansas from its early settlers to modern times, making it a must-visit for history buffs and curious minds.

Location: 200 E 3rd St, Little Rock, AR 72201-1608

Closest City or Town: Little Rock, Arkansas

How to Get There: From I-30, take exit 141A for 2nd St, turn right onto E 3rd St, and the museum will be on your left.

GPS Coordinates: 34.7460543° N, 92.2690532° W

Best Time to Visit: Year-round

Pass/Permit/Fees: Entry fees apply; check the website for details

Did You Know? The museum houses the largest collection of Arkansas-made paintings, furniture, and pottery in the state.

Website: http://www.historicarkansas.org/

Little Rock Zoo

Immerse yourself in a world of wildlife at the Little Rock Zoo, an animal lover's paradise in Little Rock, Arkansas. This family-friendly attraction houses over 500 animals representing more than 200 species and offers an exciting array of exhibits, from majestic big cats to playful primates. Situated in War Memorial Park, the zoo provides a fun, educational experience with daily animal shows, interactive exhibits, and lovely gardens. Don't miss a ride on the endangered species carousel or a voyage on the train for a delightful day out.

Location: 1 Zoo Dr, Little Rock, AR 72205-5401

Closest City or Town: Little Rock, Arkansas

How to Get There: From I-630, take the Fair Park Blvd exit and turn right, follow the signs to the zoo entrance.

GPS Coordinates: 34.7470271° N, 92.3301901° W

Best Time to Visit: Spring and fall for mild weather and active animals

Pass/Permit/Fees: Admission fees apply; visit the website for pricing.

Did You Know? The Little Rock Zoo first opened in 1926 and started with only two animals: an abandoned timber wolf and a circus-trained bear.

Website: http://www.littlerockzoo.com/

MacArthur Museum of Arkansas Military History

Step into the storied past of Arkansas's military heritage at the MacArthur Museum of Arkansas Military History in Little Rock. Set within the historic Tower Building of the Little Rock Arsenal, this museum honors the legacy of General Douglas MacArthur and other Arkansas veterans. Located in the beautiful MacArthur Park, the museum portrays compelling exhibits with artifacts, photographs, and military memorabilia. Visitors can explore the rich history of military engagements and Arkansas's role from the Civil War to contemporary conflicts.

Location: 503 E 9th St, Little Rock, AR 72202-3997

Closest City or Town: Little Rock, Arkansas

How to Get There: From I-630, take exit 2A and head east on 9th Street; the museum is located within MacArthur Park.

GPS Coordinates: 34.7383187° N, 92.2652979° W

Best Time to Visit: Year-round

Pass/Permit/Fees: Free to enter

Did You Know? The Tower Building of the Little Rock Arsenal, where the museum is situated, is one of the oldest buildings in central Arkansas, built in 1840.

Website: http://littlerock.gov/macarthur

Museum Of Discovery

Find your sense of curiosity and wonder at the Museum Of Discovery in Little Rock, Arkansas. This highly interactive museum captivates visitors of all ages with its hands-on exhibits in science, technology, engineering, and math (STEM). Located along the bustling River Market District, the museum offers an exciting escape into the world of discovery. Whether you're launching rockets, experiencing tornado simulations, or exploring the wonders of the human body, every exhibit aims to ignite a passion for learning and exploration. Special events and programs further enrich this already incredible experience.

Location: 500 President Clinton Ave, Little Rock, AR 72201-1756

Closest City or Town: Little Rock, Arkansas

How to Get There: From I-30, take Exit 141A to merge onto President Clinton Ave. The museum will be on your left in the River Market District.

GPS Coordinates: 34.7475223° N, 92.2646356° W

Best Time to Visit: Year-round

Pass/Permit/Fees: Admission fees apply; visit the website for details.

Did You Know? The Museum of Discovery is Arkansas's oldest museum, originally founded in 1927.

Website: http://www.museumofdiscovery.org/

Mystery Mansion Escape Room

Unlock your sense of adventure and puzzle-solving skills at the Mystery Mansion Escape Room in Little Rock, Arkansas. This thrilling attraction offers themed escape rooms that challenge participants to use their wits and teamwork to solve clues and escape within 60 minutes. Located in the heart of Little Rock, each room transports you into different scenarios, from haunted houses to treasure hunts, making it an unforgettable experience for friends, families, and team-building activities.

Location: 2122 S Broadway St, Little Rock, AR 72206-1356

Closest City or Town: Little Rock, Arkansas

How to Get There: From I-30, take Exit 138 B for 6th St, turn onto S Broadway St, and continue until you reach the Mystery Mansion on your right.

GPS Coordinates: 34.7279007° N, 92.2790162° W

Best Time to Visit: Year-round

Pass/Permit/Fees: Admission fees apply; visit the website for details.

Did You Know? The Mystery Mansion Escape Room offers a variety of room themes that change periodically, ensuring a new adventure with every visit.

Website: http://mysterymansionescape.com/

Old State House Museum

Delve into Arkansas's rich history at the Old State House Museum in Little Rock. This iconic landmark, originally constructed in 1836, served as the state's first capitol building. Located on West Markham Street, the museum offers a fascinating array of exhibits showcasing the cultural and political heritage of Arkansas. Visitors can explore historic artifacts, period rooms, and engaging displays that tell the story of the state from its beginnings to the present day.

Location: 300 W Markham St, Little Rock, AR 72201-1406

Closest City or Town: Little Rock, Arkansas

How to Get There: From I-30, take Exit 141A, merge onto President Clinton Ave, turn left on Main St, and right onto W Markham St to reach the museum.

GPS Coordinates: 34.7490498° N, 92.2725927° W

Best Time to Visit: Year-round

Pass/Permit/Fees: Free to enter

Did You Know? The Old State House was the site of Bill Clinton's election night celebrations for his presidential campaigns in 1992 and 1996.

Website: http://www.oldstatehouse.com/

Pinnacle Mountain State Park

Embrace the great outdoors at Pinnacle Mountain State Park, located just outside Little Rock, Arkansas. This expansive park, home to the majestic Pinnacle Mountain, offers endless recreational opportunities including hiking, mountain biking, and picnicking. Explore over 15 miles of scenic trails, ranging from easy nature walks to challenging summit trails that reward hikers with panoramic views of the Arkansas River Valley. Special programs and guided tours enhance the experience, making it a perfect destination for outdoor enthusiasts.

Location: 9600 Highway 300, Little Rock, AR 72135

Closest City or Town: Little Rock, Arkansas

How to Get There: From I-430, take Exit 9 for AR-10 W, then turn right onto AR-300 N and follow signs to the park.

GPS Coordinates: 34.8422716° N, 92.4947551° W

Best Time to Visit: Spring and fall for comfortable hiking weather

Pass/Permit/Fees: Free to enter; some activities may have fees

Did You Know? Pinnacle Mountain rises over 1,000 feet above the Arkansas River, making it a distinctive natural landmark visible from many parts of Little Rock.

Website: http://www.arkansasstateparks.com/pinnaclemountain/

River Market District

Discover the vibrant heart of Little Rock at the River Market District, a bustling hub of dining, shopping, and entertainment. Located along the Arkansas River, this dynamic area offers something for everyone, from farmers markets and food halls to art galleries and cultural experiences. Stroll along the riverfront, enjoy live music, or indulge in the diverse culinary options available. The district also hosts a variety of events and festivals, making it a lively and essential part of the city's culture.

Location: 400 President Clinton Ave, Little Rock, AR 72201-1638

Closest City or Town: Little Rock, Arkansas

How to Get There: From I-30, take Exit 141A to merge onto President Clinton Ave. The district encompasses multiple blocks along the riverfront.

GPS Coordinates: 34.7476883° N, 92.2661552° W

Best Time to Visit: Year-round; spring and summer for outdoor events

Pass/Permit/Fees: Free to explore

Did You Know? The River Market District is home to the Junction Bridge, a pedestrian bridge offering stunning views of the Arkansas River.

Website: http://www.rivermarket.info/

Riverfront Park

Find your sense of tranquility and adventure at Riverfront Park, a beautiful green space nestled along the vibrant Arkansas River in downtown Little Rock. Stretching for 33 acres, this park offers a mix of history, art, and scenic beauty, making it a perfect getaway within the urban landscape. Visitors can explore trails, play in interactive water features, admire public art, or enjoy the panoramic river views. The park also hosts festivals and community events throughout the year, adding to its lively ambiance.

Location: 400 President Clinton Ave, Little Rock, AR 72201

Closest City or Town: Little Rock, Arkansas

How to Get There: Easily accessible via Interstate 30; take exit 141A towards President Clinton Ave.

GPS Coordinates: 34.7484093° N, 92.2669120° W

Best Time to Visit: Spring through fall for the best weather and events

Pass/Permit/Fees: Free to enter

Did You Know? The park includes the Junction Bridge, a pedestrian and cyclist bridge with stunning views of the Arkansas River.

Website: https://www.littlerock.com/river-market/play/riverfront-park/

Rock Town Distillery

Step into the world of craft spirits at Rock Town Distillery, located in the heart of Little Rock, Arkansas. Established as the first legal distillery in the state since Prohibition, Rock Town offers a unique tasting experience with its award-winning selection of bourbons, vodkas, and gins. Visitors can tour the facility to learn about the distillation process, sample different spirits, and even purchase bottles to take home.

Location: 1201 Main St, Little Rock, AR 72202-5031

Closest City or Town: Little Rock, Arkansas

How to Get There: From I-630, take exit 2A and head south on Main Street until you reach the distillery.

GPS Coordinates: 34.7369930° N, 92.2720862° W

Best Time to Visit: Year-round

Pass/Permit/Fees: Fees apply for tours and tastings

Did You Know? Rock Town sources all of its grains within 125 miles of the distillery, supporting local agriculture.

Simmons Bank Arena

Catch a concert, cheer at a sports event, or be mesmerized by a Broadway show at Simmons Bank Arena, a premier entertainment venue in North Little Rock, Arkansas. Overlooking the Arkansas River, this state-of-the-art arena hosts a variety of performances and events, drawing visitors from all over. With a seating capacity of up to 18,000, it offers a fantastic viewing experience for every guest, ensuring every event is unforgettable.

Location: 1 Simmons Bank Arena Dr, Little Rock, AR 72114-5681

Closest City or Town: Little Rock, Arkansas

How to Get There: Accessible via I-30; take exit 141A towards Broadway St.

GPS Coordinates: 34.7549640° N, 92.2644730° W

Best Time to Visit: Year-round; check their schedule for events

Pass/Permit/Fees: Event ticket prices vary

Did You Know? The arena was originally named Alltel Arena and opened in 1999.

Website: http://simmonsbankarena.com/

The Arkansas River Trail

Embark on a scenic journey along The Arkansas River Trail, a renowned 88-mile loop that connects Little Rock and North Little Rock. This multi-use trail offers breathtaking views of the Arkansas River, historic landmarks, and verdant parks. Perfect for biking, jogging, or a leisurely walk, it's a great way to explore the local landscape and engage in outdoor activities. The trail also features several access points, making it easily accessible for everyone.

Location: 400 President Clinton Ave, Little Rock River Market, Little Rock, AR 72201-1638

Closest City or Town: Little Rock, Arkansas

How to Get There: Starting from downtown Little Rock, head towards the River Market District.

GPS Coordinates: 34.7476319° N, 92.2661051° W

Best Time to Visit: Spring through fall for the best outdoor conditions

Pass/Permit/Fees: Free to access

Did You Know? The trail loops around the river, passing through 38 parks and six distinct districts.

Website: http://arkansasrivertrail.org/

Two Rivers Park

Discover a lush green escape at Two Rivers Park, situated at the confluence of the Arkansas and Little Maumelle Rivers in Little Rock, Arkansas. This scenic park offers over 1,000 acres of meadows, wetlands, and woodlands, perfect for picnicking, hiking, biking, and wildlife observation. Explore the paved trails, enjoy the serenity of the natural surroundings, or relax by the rivers.

Location: RH6X+QC, 6900 Two Rivers Park Road, Little Rock, AR 72223

Closest City or Town: Little Rock, Arkansas

How to Get There: From I-430, take exit 9 and follow signs to Cantrell Rd, then turn onto Two Rivers Park Road.

GPS Coordinates: 34.8122896° N, 92.4020922° W

Best Time to Visit: Spring through fall

Pass/Permit/Fees: Free to enter

Did You Know? Two Rivers Park features a 450-foot-long pedestrian bridge that connects the park to the Arkansas River Trail.

Website: https://pulaskicounty.net/two-rivers-park/

MAMMOTH SPRING

Mammoth Spring State Park

Find your sense of tranquility and history at Mammoth Spring State Park, one of Arkansas's natural treasures. Located in Mammoth Spring, this park is built around a breathtaking spring that flows at an average rate of nine million gallons per hour, creating Spring River. Explore serene walking trails, visit the 1886 Frisco Depot Museum, and picnic beside the picturesque spring lake. The park's unique feature is the chance to see and learn about one of the largest springs in the nation, offering an unforgettable outdoor experience.

Location: U.S. 63, Mammoth Spring, AR 72554

Closest City or Town: Mammoth Spring, Arkansas

How to Get There: Easily accessible via U.S. Highway 63, situated in the heart of Mammoth Spring.

GPS Coordinates: 36.4957993° N, 91.5355124° W

Best Time to Visit: Spring through fall to enjoy mild weather and lush scenery

Pass/Permit/Fees: Free to enter; some activities may have fees

Did You Know? Mammoth Spring is one of the world's largest springs, gushing around nine million gallons of water per hour.

Website: http://www.arkansasstateparks.com/mammothspring

MENA

Board Camp Crystal Mine

Delve into the fascinating world of minerals at Board Camp Crystal Mine, a unique attraction in Mena, Arkansas. This open-air mine allows visitors to dig for their own crystals, providing an exciting and hands-on experience. Marvel at the stunning natural formations and enjoy the thrill of finding your own sparkling treasures. The mine also offers guided tours and night digs, making it a perfect adventure for the entire family.

Location: 110 Polk Road 62, Mena, AR 71953-8346

Closest City or Town: Mena, Arkansas

How to Get There: From U.S. Highway 71 in Mena, take AR-88 W to Polk Road 62 and follow signs to the mine.

GPS Coordinates: 34.5365830° N, 94.0910830° W

Best Time to Visit: Spring through fall for pleasant weather

Pass/Permit/Fees: Admission fees apply for mining activities

Did You Know? The crystals at Board Camp Crystal Mine are renowned for their clarity and beauty.

Website: http://www.boardcampcrystalmine.com/

Queen Wilhelmina State Park

Ascend to new heights at Queen Wilhelmina State Park, situated atop Rich Mountain, the second highest peak in Arkansas. Located in Mena, this park offers stunning vistas, pristine hiking trails, and a historic lodge with luxurious accommodations. Enjoy outdoor activities such as picnicking, birdwatching, and exploring the scenic Talimena National Scenic Byway. The park's unique highlight is its rich history, initially established as a Victorian resort in the late 19th century.

Location: 3877 Highway 88 W, Mena, AR 71953-8317

Closest City or Town: Mena, Arkansas

How to Get There: From U.S. Highway 71, follow AR-88 W, also known as the Talimena Scenic Drive, to reach the park.

GPS Coordinates: 34.6858036° N, 94.3715585° W

Best Time to Visit: Spring and fall for the best foliage and mild temperatures

Pass/Permit/Fees: Free to enter; lodging and some activities have fees

Did You Know? Queen Wilhelmina State Park Lodge is named after the Queen of the Netherlands, reflecting its European influence.

Website: http://www.queenwilhelmina.com/

MORRILTON

Cedar Falls Trail

Experience the natural beauty of Cedar Falls Trail, a must-visit hiking destination located within Petit Jean State Park in Morrilton, Arkansas. This scenic trail leads to the awe-inspiring Cedar Falls, plunging over 90 feet into Cedar Creek. Hike through lush forests, over rugged terrain, and witness the breathtaking waterfall – a perfect spot for nature photography and relaxation. The trail offers a rewarding and invigorating experience, capturing the essence of Arkansas's natural splendor.

Location: Exit No. 108 off I-40 at Morrilton, Petit Jean State Park, Morrilton, AR 72110

Closest City or Town: Morrilton, Arkansas

How to Get There: From I-40, take Exit 108 and follow AR-9 S and AR-154 W to Petit Jean State Park.

GPS Coordinates: 35.6473757° N, 82.0378828° W

Best Time to Visit: Spring for the fullest waterfall flow

Pass/Permit/Fees: Free to hike

Did You Know? Cedar Falls is among the most photographed natural landmarks in Arkansas.

Website: http://www.petitjeanstatepark.com/things_to_do/trails-detail.aspx?id=35

Petit Jean State Park

Find your sense of adventure in the heart of Arkansas at Petit Jean State Park, the state's first and most beautiful state park. Located in Morrilton, this park offers a plethora of outdoor activities from hiking and camping to fishing and boating. Explore captivating trails, visit the mysterious Petit Jean's gravesite and marvel at dramatic overlooks. The park's unique draw is its rich Native American history and stunning natural features that captivate every visitor.

ARKANSAS BUCKET LIST

Location: 1285 Petit Jean Mountain Rd, Morrilton, AR 72110-9361

Closest City or Town: Morrilton, Arkansas

How to Get There: From I-40, take Exit 108 and follow AR-9 S to AR-154 W towards Petit Jean Mountain Rd.

GPS Coordinates: 35.1242439° N, 92.9234759° W

Best Time to Visit: Spring and fall for pleasant weather and vibrant foliage

Pass/Permit/Fees: Free to enter; lodging and some activities have fees

Did You Know? The park is named after Petit Jean, a young French woman who disguised herself as a boy to follow her lover to America.

Website: http://petitjeanstatepark.com/

MOUNT IDA

Twin Creek Crystal Mine

Unearth your sense of adventure at Twin Creek Crystal Mine, situated amidst the scenic hills of Mount Ida, Arkansas. This gem of a destination lets visitors dig their own crystals directly from the rich Arkansas soil. Located on Collier Springs Road, the mine offers an incredible hands-on experience where you can unearth beautiful quartz crystals while basking in the natural splendor of the Ouachita Mountains. This is a treasure hunt in the truest sense, perfect for families and gem enthusiasts alike.

Location: Collier Springs Road Rd #177, Mount Ida, AR 71957-8266

Closest City or Town: Mount Ida, Arkansas

How to Get There: From Mount Ida, take Highway 270 west towards Pencil Bluff, then turn right onto Owley Road and follow signs to Collier Springs Road.

GPS Coordinates: 34.4991283° N, 93.5671107° W

Best Time to Visit: Spring and fall for comfortable outdoor conditions

Pass/Permit/Fees: Fees for digging; check the website for details

Did You Know? Mount Ida is known as the Quartz Crystal Capital of the World due to its rich deposits.

Website: https://www.facebook.com/p/Twin-Creek-Crystal-Mine-100090278926830/

Wegner Quartz Crystal Mines

Experience the thrill of discovery at Wegner Quartz Crystal Mines in Mount Ida, Arkansas. Located just off Wegner Crystal Ranch Road, this mining facility invites you to hunt for stunning quartz crystals amidst the rugged beauty of the Ouachita Mountains. Engage in a variety of activities, from guided tours to seasonal mining digs, each providing a unique glimpse into Arkansas's natural treasures. As you sift through the earth, you'll find an array of crystals, making every visit an exciting and rewarding adventure.

ARKANSAS BUCKET LIST

Location: 82 Wegner Crystal Ranch Rd, Mount Ida, AR 71957-8600

Closest City or Town: Mount Ida, Arkansas

How to Get There: From Mount Ida, head west on Highway 270, then follow signs to North Crystal Vista Road, merging onto Wegner Crystal Ranch Road.

GPS Coordinates: 34.5141271° N, 93.6411858° W

Best Time to Visit: Spring and fall for mild weather and active digging

Pass/Permit/Fees: Fees for mining; details on the website

Did You Know? Wegner Quartz Crystal Mines offers a rare Tailings Dig experience, where you can search through previously mined materials for hidden gems.

Website:
https://www.geology.arkansas.gov/docs/pdf/education/arkansas-quartz-crystals.pdf

MOUNT IDA

Lake Ouachita

Discover endless outdoor adventures at Lake Ouachita, a pristine reservoir nestled in the Ouachita National Forest near Mountain Pine, Arkansas. With over 200 islands and 975 miles of shoreline, it's the largest lake entirely within Arkansas. Visitors can indulge in activities like boating, fishing, swimming, and scuba diving in some of the cleanest freshwater lakes in the country. The surrounding park offers scenic trails for hiking and biking, ensuring there's something for every nature enthusiast.

Location: 5451 Mountain Pine Rd, Mountain Pine, AR 71956-9709

Closest City or Town: Mountain Pine, Arkansas

How to Get There: From Hot Springs, take Highway 270 west, then turn right onto Mountain Pine Road and follow signs to the marina.

GPS Coordinates: 34.6325810° N, 93.1646360° W

Best Time to Visit: Summer for water activities; fall for hiking and foliage views

Pass/Permit/Fees: Entrance fees may apply for certain activities; see the website for details

Did You Know? Lake Ouachita is renowned for its water clarity and has numerous dive sites for underwater exploration.

Website: https://www.recreation.gov/camping/gateways/147

MOUNTAIN VIEW

Blanchard Springs Recreation Area

Find your sense of wonder at Blanchard Springs Recreation Area, located in the lush Ozark National Forest near Mountain View, Arkansas. This natural oasis offers stunning underground tours of the Blanchard Springs Caverns, pristine hiking trails, and the scenic Blanchard Springs waterfall. Visitors can enjoy picnicking, swimming, and fishing in Mirror Lake, creating an ideal setting for a day of outdoor adventure and relaxation amidst awe-inspiring natural beauty.

Location: Forest Service Road 1110, Mountain View, AR 72560

Closest City or Town: Mountain View, Arkansas

How to Get There: From Mountain View, take Highway 14 west and follow the signs to the recreation area.

GPS Coordinates: 35.9692084° N, 92.1735359° W

Best Time to Visit: Spring through fall when the weather is pleasant and trails are in full bloom

Pass/Permit/Fees: Fees apply for cavern tours; see the website for details

Did You Know? Blanchard Springs Caverns is one of the most carefully developed caves in the country, preserving its natural beauty while making it accessible for visitors.

Website:
http://www.fs.fed.us/oonf/ozark/recreation/blanchard.html

Ozark Folk Center State Park

Immerse yourself in the rich cultural heritage of the Ozarks at the Ozark Folk Center State Park in Mountain View, Arkansas. This living history park celebrates the music, crafts, and traditions of the Ozark region. Wander through workshops where artisans demonstrate traditional crafts, enjoy live folk music performances, and explore the native herb garden. The center's rustic setting provides an authentic look into the past, making it a unique cultural experience for visitors of all ages.

Location: 1032 Park Ave, Mountain View, AR 72560-6008

Closest City or Town: Mountain View, Arkansas

How to Get There: From Mountain View, take Highway 9 north and turn left onto Park Avenue.

GPS Coordinates: 35.8818690° N, 92.1155061° W

Best Time to Visit: Spring and fall for events and workshops

Pass/Permit/Fees: Entrance fees apply; visit the website for details

Did You Know? The Ozark Folk Center is the only park in the US dedicated to preserving the Ozark way of life through interactive exhibits and live demonstrations.

Website: http://www.ozarkfolkcenter.com/

MOUNTAINBURG

Lake Fort Smith State Park

Find your sense of adventure and tranquility at Lake Fort Smith State Park, nestled in the scenic Boston Mountains of Arkansas. This beautiful park offers visitors a plethora of outdoor activities, from hiking on picturesque trails to boating and fishing on the serene Lake Fort Smith. The park provides a perfect escape with its campgrounds, picnic areas, and a well-equipped visitor center.

Location: 15458 Shepherd Spring Rd, Mountainburg, AR 72946-4020

Closest City or Town: Mountainburg, Arkansas

How to Get There: From I-540, take exit 29 for AR-282 W towards Mountainburg. Follow the signs to the state park.

GPS Coordinates: 35.6959506° N, 94.1188313° W

Best Time to Visit: Spring through fall for the best weather and outdoor activities

Pass/Permit/Fees: Park entry is free; fees apply for camping and certain activities

Did You Know? The park's visitor center has exhibits on the 1930s Civilian Conservation Corps who originally built the park.

Website: http://www.arkansasstateparks.com/lakefortsmith/

MURFREESBORO

Ka Do Ha Indian Village

Venture into the ancient past at Ka Do Ha Indian Village, an archaeological treasure trove in Murfreesboro, Arkansas. This historical site invites visitors to explore the remnants of a prehistoric Native American village, offering unique experiences such as artifact digging, museum tours, and educational programs.

Location: 281 Kadoha Rd, Murfreesboro, AR 71958-8808

Closest City or Town: Murfreesboro, Arkansas

How to Get There: Accessible via AR-27 S; follow signs from Murfreesboro to Kadoha Road.

GPS Coordinates: 34.0615252° N, 93.7182021° W

Best Time to Visit: Spring and fall for mild weather

Pass/Permit/Fees: Admission fees apply

Did You Know? Ka Do Ha features a hands-on dig site where visitors can search for authentic, buried artifacts.

Website: http://www.kadoha.com/

NORTH LITTLE ROCK

Arkansas Inland Maritime Museum

Dive into naval history at the Arkansas Inland Maritime Museum in North Little Rock, Arkansas. This fascinating museum is home to the USS Razorback, a World War II submarine, and offers immersive tours that delve into the life of submariners. Visitors can explore other naval artifacts and exhibits, making it an educational and thrilling experience for all.

Location: 120 Riverfront Park Dr, North Little Rock, AR 72114-5640

Closest City or Town: North Little Rock, Arkansas

How to Get There: From I-30, take Exit 141A towards Broadway St and follow signs to Riverfront Park Dr.

GPS Coordinates: 34.7522251° N, 92.2669543° W

Best Time to Visit: Year-round

Pass/Permit/Fees: Admission fees apply

Did You Know? The USS Razorback participated in the surrender ceremony of World War II in Tokyo Bay.

Website: http://aimmuseum.org/

Burns Park

Discover a recreational paradise at Burns Park, one of the largest municipal parks in America, located in North Little Rock, Arkansas. Spanning 1,700 acres, the park offers a wide array of activities including hiking, biking, golfing, disc golf, and a delightful amusement park. Ideal for family outings and sports enthusiasts, Burns Park promises endless fun and relaxation.

Location: 4400 Funland, North Little Rock, AR 72118

Closest City or Town: North Little Rock, Arkansas

How to Get There: From I-40, take Exit 150 and follow signs to Burns Park.

GPS Coordinates: 34.7976957° N, 92.3099177° W

Best Time to Visit: Spring through fall for optimal outdoor activities

Pass/Permit/Fees: Free to enter; some amenities may have fees

Did You Know? Burns Park features a covered bridge built in 1872, one of the few remaining in Arkansas.

Website: http://nlrpr.org/cms/one.aspx?portalId=96195&pageId=96854

Dickey-Stephens Park

Catch a game and cheer for the home team at Dickey-Stephens Park, the charming baseball stadium in North Little Rock, Arkansas. Home to the Arkansas Travelers, this family-friendly venue offers classic ballpark snacks, scenic views of downtown Little Rock, and an electric atmosphere that makes every game special.

Location: 400 W Broadway St, North Little Rock, AR 72114-5522

Closest City or Town: North Little Rock, Arkansas

How to Get There: From I-30, take Exit 141A for Broadway St, and the park will be on your left.

GPS Coordinates: 34.7554963° N, 92.2725633° W

Best Time to Visit: During the baseball season, typically spring through summer

Pass/Permit/Fees: Ticket prices vary by game

Did You Know? Dickey-Stephens Park is named after four individuals: Bill Dickey, Skeeter Dickey, Jack Stephens, and Witt Stephens.

Website: http://www.milb.com/

Junction Bridge

Explore the historical charm and modern flair of Junction Bridge, an iconic pedestrian bridge spanning the Arkansas River in North Little Rock, Arkansas. Originally a railway bridge, it now serves as a scenic walkway, offering breathtaking views of the river and city skyline. This accessible bridge connects visitors to various attractions on both sides of the river, providing a unique vantage point for photo opportunities and quiet moments of contemplation.

Location: 200 E Washington Ave, North Little Rock, AR 72114

Closest City or Town: North Little Rock, Arkansas

How to Get There: From downtown Little Rock, take the River Market District route towards President Clinton Ave, and follow signs to Junction Bridge.

GPS Coordinates: 34.7538138° N, 92.2664614° W

Best Time to Visit: Spring and summer for the best weather and river views

Pass/Permit/Fees: Free to access

Did You Know? Junction Bridge was part of the original route of the Rock Island Railroad and was transformed into a pedestrian bridge in 2008.

Website: https://en.wikipedia.org/wiki/Arkansas_River_Trail

The Old Mill

Step back in time at The Old Mill, a picturesque replica of an 1880s water-powered grist mill, located in the serene setting of T.R. Pugh Memorial Park in North Little Rock. This enchanting destination, featured in the opening scene of the classic film Gone with the Wind, is adorned with rustic bridges, charming sculptures, and lush greenery, making it ideal for leisurely strolls, photography, and peaceful reflection.

Location: 3800 Lakeshore Dr T.R. Pugh Memorial Park, North Little Rock, AR 72116

Closest City or Town: North Little Rock, Arkansas

How to Get There: From downtown Little Rock, take I-30 N and exit onto AR-161 N/Broadway St. Continue on Main St, then turn left onto Lakeshore Dr.

GPS Coordinates: 34.7917000° N, 92.2494000° W

Best Time to Visit: Spring and fall for pleasant weather and vibrant foliage

Pass/Permit/Fees: Free to enter

Did You Know? The Old Mill is believed to be the only remaining structure from Gone with the Wind that still stands today.

Website: http://northlittlerock.org/attractions_detail/285

ODEN

Ouachita National Forest

Find your sense of adventure in the vast expanse of Ouachita National Forest, spanning over 1.8 million acres across Arkansas and Oklahoma. This pristine forest offers a rich tapestry of recreational activities, including hiking, biking, fishing, and camping. Experience the thrill of exploring scenic trails, taking in the breathtaking vistas, and discovering the diverse flora and fauna that thrive in this natural haven.

Location: M5MP+RG, Oden, AR 71961

Closest City or Town: Oden, Arkansas

How to Get There: From Hot Springs, take US-270 W towards Mount Ida, then continue on AR-88 W until you reach the forest.

GPS Coordinates: 34.6845625° N, 93.8136875° W

Best Time to Visit: Spring and fall for ideal hiking and camping weather

Pass/Permit/Fees: Free to enter; some activities may have fees

Did You Know? Ouachita National Forest is one of the oldest national forests in the southern United States, established in 1907.

Website: https://www.fs.usda.gov/main/ouachita/home

PARIS

Mount Magazine State Park

Unleash your adventurous spirit at Mount Magazine State Park, home to the highest point in Arkansas. This park in Paris, Arkansas offers a wealth of activities such as hiking, hang gliding, rock climbing, and wildlife watching. The scenic trails lead you through diverse terrains, providing stunning views of the Arkansas River Valley. Whether you visit for the day or stay in the luxurious lodge, you will be immersed in nature's grandeur.

Location: 16878 Highway 309 South, Paris, AR 72855

Closest City or Town: Paris, Arkansas

How to Get There: From I-40, take exit 78 for AR-22 W towards Paris. Continue on AR-309 S to reach the park.

GPS Coordinates: 35.1686949° N, 93.6260549° W

Best Time to Visit: Spring and fall for the best foliage and mild temperatures

Pass/Permit/Fees: Free to enter; lodging and some activities have fees

Did You Know? Mount Magazine's summit is 2,753 feet above sea level, making it the tallest mountain in Arkansas.

Website: https://www.arkansasstateparks.com/parks/mount-magazine-state-park

PRAIRIE GROVE

Prairie Grove Battlefield State Park

Journey back to the Civil War era at Prairie Grove Battlefield State Park, the site of one of the last major battles west of the Mississippi River. Located in Prairie Grove, Arkansas, this park offers a deep dive into history with interpretive programs, guided tours, and a museum exhibiting artifacts from the battle. Walk among the preserved battlefield grounds and imagine the pivotal moments of the 1862 conflict.

Location: 14262 W Highway 62, Prairie Grove, AR 72753-2731

Closest City or Town: Prairie Grove, Arkansas

How to Get There: From Fayetteville, take US-62 W towards Prairie Grove. The park is located just off the highway.

GPS Coordinates: 35.9831194° N, 94.3106300° W

Best Time to Visit: Spring and fall for optimal weather; special reenactments in December

Pass/Permit/Fees: Free to enter

Did You Know? The Battle of Prairie Grove ensured Union control over northwest Arkansas, a pivotal moment in the Civil War.

Website:
http://www.arkansasstateparks.com/prairiegrovebattlefield

ROGERS

Daisy Airgun Museum

Journey back in time at the Daisy Airgun Museum, an iconic destination located in Rogers, Arkansas. This fascinating museum chronicles the history of the airgun, showcasing a treasure trove of vintage airguns and memorabilia. Visitors can explore the extensive exhibits detailing the evolution of Daisy airguns from the late 1800s to today. Located in the heart of Rogers, this museum offers a nostalgic experience, evoking the adventurous spirit of childhood through interactive displays and historical artifacts. The unique feature here is the collection of the rare and iconic Red Ryder BB gun, a cultural icon for many.

Location: 202 W Walnut St, Rogers, AR 72756-6665

Closest City or Town: Rogers, Arkansas

How to Get There: From Interstate 49, take exit 85 and head east on Walnut Street until you reach the museum.

GPS Coordinates: 36.3329937° N, 94.1176025° W

Best Time to Visit: Year-round

Pass/Permit/Fees: Admission fees apply; check the website for details.

Did You Know? The museum houses the original Plymouth Iron Windmill Company, which became the Daisy Manufacturing Company in 1895.

Website: http://www.daisymuseum.com/

Hobbs State Park Conservation Area

Find your sense of serenity and adventure at Hobbs State Park Conservation Area, located near Rogers, Arkansas. This expansive park, the largest of its kind in Arkansas, offers over 12,000 acres of beautiful Ozark landscapes and outdoor activities. Visitors can hike or bike along 36 miles of trails, paddle on the Beaver Lake, or explore interactive exhibits at the visitor center. Nestled in the Ozark

Mountains, Hobbs State Park is a paradise for nature lovers and outdoor enthusiasts alike, with its distinctive karst landscapes and pristine natural beauty.

Location: 20201 E Highway 12, Rogers, AR 72756-7530

Closest City or Town: Rogers, Arkansas

How to Get There: From Highway 12, heading east out of Rogers, follow signs to the park entrance.

GPS Coordinates: 36.2859260° N, 93.9390280° W

Best Time to Visit: Spring through fall

Pass/Permit/Fees: Free to enter; some activities may have fees

Did You Know? The park includes the Historic Van Winkle Trail, which leads to the remnants of an 1870s-era homestead and mill site.

Website:
http://www.arkansasstateparks.com/hobbsstateparkconservationarea/#.UaTJhtLVDh4

War Eagle Cavern on Beaver Lake

Embark on an underground adventure at War Eagle Cavern on Beaver Lake, a stunning natural attraction in Rogers, Arkansas. This sprawling cavern features guided tours that delve into its intricate formations and mysterious passages. Nestled along the shores of the picturesque Beaver Lake, visitors can enjoy scenic boat tours, hike along the adjacent nature trails, and pan for gems. Unique for its underground wonder, the cavern offers a captivating glimpse into Arkansas' geological history.

Location: 21494 Cavern Drive, Rogers, AR 72756-7493

Closest City or Town: Rogers, Arkansas

How to Get There: From downtown Rogers, head east on Highway 12, then follow the signs for War Eagle Cavern.

GPS Coordinates: 36.2952521° N, 93.9044702° W

Best Time to Visit: Spring through fall

Pass/Permit/Fees: Admission fees apply; see the website for specifics.

Did You Know? War Eagle Cavern is home to one of the largest colonies of pipistrelle bats in the region.

Website: http://www.wareaglecavern.com/

War Eagle Mill General Store

Discover a slice of history at War Eagle Mill General Store, a historic working mill located in Rogers, Arkansas. This charming establishment invites visitors to witness traditional milling processes as they watch water-powered grinding of organic grains. Positioned along the beautiful War Eagle Creek, the store offers locally crafted goods and freshly baked delights. The mill provides a unique blend of history, culture, and natural beauty, offering a glimpse into Arkansas' past while creating an inviting shopping experience.

Location: 11045 War Eagle Rd, Rogers, AR 72756-7544

Closest City or Town: Rogers, Arkansas

How to Get There: From downtown Rogers, take Highway 12 east, then turn onto War Eagle Road and follow until you reach the mill.

GPS Coordinates: 36.2672727° N, 93.9431532° W

Best Time to Visit: Spring and fall for the best experience

Pass/Permit/Fees: Free to enter; fees for certain events or activities

Did You Know? The mill has been operating since 1832 and has been rebuilt three times after floods and fires.

Website: http://www.visitwareaglemill.com/

P. Allen Smith's Garden Home

Step into a world of botanical beauty at P. Allen Smith's Garden Home, located at Moss Mountain Farm in Roland, Arkansas. This stunning garden home, designed by renowned horticulturalist P. Allen Smith, showcases the best of Southern gardening and design. Visitors can tour the exquisite house, walk through the terraced gardens, and explore the farm's sustainable practices. Set against the backdrop of the Arkansas River, the Garden Home offers a blend of elegance, functionality, and environmental stewardship, providing inspiration for gardeners and nature lovers alike.

ARKANSAS BUCKET LIST

Location: Ross Hollow Road Moss Mountain Farm, Roland, AR 72135

Closest City or Town: Roland, Arkansas

How to Get There: From Little Rock, take Highway 10 west, then follow signs to Roland and Moss Mountain Farm.

GPS Coordinates: 34.9373426° N, 92.5134767° W

Best Time to Visit: Spring through fall for the best garden views

Pass/Permit/Fees: Admission fees apply; visit the website for details.

Did You Know? Moss Mountain Farm is also home to heritage livestock breeds, contributing to agricultural biodiversity.

Website: http://www.pallensmith.com/garden-home-retreat/visit

RUSSELLVILLE

Lake Dardenelle State Park

Discover the natural beauty and outdoor adventures at Lake Dardenelle State Park, a haven for water enthusiasts and nature lovers alike. Located in Russellville, this park is set along the shores of the stunning 34,300-acre Lake Dardenelle. Visitors can enjoy activities such as fishing, kayaking, birdwatching, and hiking along scenic trails. The park also offers modern campsites and picnic areas, perfect for a family getaway. Unique features include an interpretive center and fish hatchery, providing educational exhibits and programs that delve into the local ecosystem.

Location: 100 State Park Dr, Russellville, AR 72802-8546

Closest City or Town: Russellville, Arkansas

How to Get There: From I-40, take Exit 81 for AR-7 S towards Russellville. Follow AR-7 S and signs to Lake Dardenelle State Park.

GPS Coordinates: 35.2829931° N, 93.2029827° W

Best Time to Visit: Spring through fall for the best outdoor activities

Pass/Permit/Fees: Free to enter; some activities may have fees

Did You Know? Lake Dardenelle is known for its exceptional bass fishing, attracting anglers from across the country.

Website: http://www.arkansasstateparks.com/lakedardanelle

SPRINGDALE

Arvest Ballpark

Experience the thrill of America's favorite pastime at Arvest Ballpark, the premier destination for sports enthusiasts in Springdale, Arkansas. Home to the Northwest Arkansas Naturals, this modern ballpark provides an electric atmosphere for baseball games. Visitors can enjoy a range of activities, from catching a game with friends and family to participating in themed events and promotions. Arvest Ballpark also features a kids' zone, picnic areas, and top-notch concessions, ensuring a fantastic day out.

Location: 3000 S 56th St, Springdale, AR 72762-0846

Closest City or Town: Springdale, Arkansas

How to Get There: From I-49, take Exit 72 for US-412 W/Sunset Ave. Turn left onto S 56th St and follow signs to Arvest Ballpark.

GPS Coordinates: 36.1596679° N, 94.1946182° W

Best Time to Visit: Spring through summer during the baseball season

Pass/Permit/Fees: Ticket prices vary depending on the game

Did You Know? Arvest Ballpark includes a Hall of Fame suite that showcases memorabilia from the rich history of the Naturals and their major league affiliates.

Website:
http://web.minorleaguebaseball.com/team1/page.jsp?ymd=20061215&content_id=148900&vkey=team1_t1350&fext=.jsp&sid=t1350

Sassafras Springs Vineyard

Indulge in a delightful escape at Sassafras Springs Vineyard, a beautiful winery located in Springdale, Arkansas. Set amidst lush landscapes, this vineyard offers an enchanting retreat for wine lovers. You can stroll through the picturesque grounds, savor a variety of locally crafted wines in the tasting room, or host a special event in the charming chapel and reception area. The idyllic setting and exceptional hospitality create an unforgettable experience.

Location: 6461 E Guy Terry Rd, Springdale, AR 72764

Closest City or Town: Springdale, Arkansas

How to Get There: From US-412, head west and turn right onto AR-265 N. Continue on Guy Terry Rd until you reach Sassafras Springs Vineyard.

GPS Coordinates: 36.1273342° N, 94.0652706° W

Best Time to Visit: Spring and fall for the most pleasant weather and vineyard events

Pass/Permit/Fees: Fees for wine tastings; see website for details

Did You Know? Sassafras Springs Vineyard hosts a variety of events, including live music, wine pairings, and special-themed dinners.

Website: http://www.sassafrasspringsvineyard.com/

Tontitown Winery

Step into a world of rich heritage and fine wine at Tontitown Winery, located in the historic town of Tontitown, near Springdale, Arkansas. Set in a beautiful, century-old building that once housed the Taldo House, this family-operated winery invites visitors to taste a selection of wines made from locally grown grapes. Enjoy a relaxing afternoon in the tasting room or explore the picturesque grounds. The winery's unique history and welcoming atmosphere make it a must-visit destination.

Location: 335 N Barrington Rd, Springdale, AR 72762-9747

Closest City or Town: Springdale, Arkansas

How to Get There: From I-49, take Exit 72 and follow US-412 W to Tontitown. Turn right onto N Barrington Rd and follow signs to Tontitown Winery.

GPS Coordinates: 36.1798660° N, 94.2350702° W

Best Time to Visit: Year-round, with special events in the spring and fall

Pass/Permit/Fees: Fees for wine tastings; see website for details

Did You Know? Tontitown has a rich Italian heritage, reflected in the winery's celebration of traditional winemaking techniques.

Website: http://www.tontitownwinery.com/

St Joe

Buffalo National River Park

Embark on an adventure in the great outdoors at the Buffalo National River Park, a stunning natural treasure in Arkansas. Begin your journey at the Tyler Bend Campground, located in St Joe. The park offers activities such as hiking along scenic trails, canoeing and kayaking on the pristine river, camping under the stars, and wildlife viewing. The unique feature of this park is its status as the first national river in the United States.

Location: 170 Ranger Rd, St Joe, AR 72675

Closest City or Town: St Joe, Arkansas

How to Get There: From US-65, take AR-14 W towards St Joe, and follow signs to Tyler Bend Campground.

GPS Coordinates: 35.9828912° N, 92.7548041° W

Best Time to Visit: Spring through fall for the best river conditions and comfortable weather

Pass/Permit/Fees: Fees apply for camping; other activities may have fees

Did You Know? The Buffalo National River is one of the few remaining undammed rivers in the lower 48 states.

Website: https://www.nps.gov/buff/planyourvisit/tyler-bend-campground.htm

MAP

We have devised an interactive map that includes all destinations described in the book.

Upon scanning a provided QR code, a link will be sent to your email, allowing you access to this unique digital feature.

This map is both detailed and user-friendly, marking every location described within the pages of the book. It provides accurate addresses and GPS coordinates for each location, coupled with direct links to the websites of these stunning destinations.

Once you receive your email link and access the interactive map, you'll have an immediate and comprehensive overview of each site's location. This invaluable tool simplifies trip planning and navigation, making it a crucial asset for both first-time visitors and seasoned explorers of Washington.

Scan the following QR or type in the provided link to receive it:

https://jo.my/arkansasbucketlistbonus

You will receive an email with links to access the Interactive Map. If you do not see our email, please look for it in spam or another section of your inbox.

In case you have any problems, you can write us at
TravelBucketList@becrepress.com

Made in the USA
Coppell, TX
16 December 2024

42843629R00066